Architectural Design

New Babylonians

Edited by Iain Borden + Sandy McCreery

 WILEY-ACADEMY

Architectural Design
Vol 71 No 3 June 2001

ISBN 0-471-49909-9
Profile No 151

Photo Credits
_AD_ Architectural Design

Abbreviated positions
b=bottom, c=centre, l=left, r=right, t=top

Cover: Courtesy Lorenzo Romito, © Stalker

p 4 photo: © Julia Chance; pp 6 courtesy Tim Brennan, photo: Gary Kirkham; pp 8 & 10 courtesy Gemeentemuseum, Den Haag 2000 c/o Beeldrecht Amstelveen, © Constant Nieuwenhuys; p 15 © Constant Nieuwenhuys; p 17 courtesy Gemeentemuseum, Den Haag 2000 c/o Beeldrecht Amstelveen, © Constant Nieuwenhuys; pp 20–22 courtesy Lorenzo Romito, © Stalker; pp 24–29 photos: © Charles Rice; pp 30–33 © Carlos Villaneuva Brandt; p 34 © Henrik Rothe and Ole Scheeren; pp 36–7, 38, 39, 40, 41 & 43 courtesy West 8, photo: © Jerden Musch; p 42 photo: © Julia Chance; pp 44–7 © General Lighting and Power; pp 48–51 courtesy Tim Brennan, photos: Gary Kirkham; pp 52–55, photos: © Laura Ruggieri; pp 56–59 © Jonathan Hill; pp 60–63 photos: © Julieanna Preston and Steven Marriott Lloyd; pp 64–67 courtesy Zoo, photos: © Andrew Lee; p 68 courtesy the Jerde Partnership Inc, photo: Benny Chan; p 69(l) photo: © Karin Jaschke; p 69(c) photo provided by George M Raymond Co, © The Raymond Group; p 69(r) photo: © Karin Jaschke; p 70(l) courtesy the Jerde Partnership Inc, photo: Hiroyuki Kawano; p 70(r) courtesy the Jerde Partnership Inc, photo: Timothy Hursley; p 71(l) photo: © Karin Jaschke; p 71(c) photo: © Karin Jaschke; p 71(l) courtesy the Jerde Partnership Inc, sketch by Jon Adams Jerde; p 73 courtesy the Jerde Partnership Inc, photo: Charles LeNoir; pp 74–77 © Stephen Tierney; pp 78–81 courtesy Barry Curtis; pp 82–87 © Gil Doron.

_AD_+
pp 94–8 courtesy Battle McCarthy; p 96(tbr) elevation of Haute Vallée School, photo: © Peter Durant/arcblue.com; p 96 photos of Rare Headquarters photo: © Dennis Gilbert/View; pp 99–103 courtesy Ove Arup; pp 104–107 © Bas Princen; p 111 courtesy Future Systems.

Subscription Offices UK
John Wiley & Sons Ltd.
Journals Administration Department
1 Oldlands Way, Bognor Regis
West Sussex, PO22 9SA
T: +44 (0)1243 843272
F: +44 (0)1243 843232
E: cs-journals@wiley.co.uk

Subscription Offices USA and Canada
John Wiley & Sons Ltd.
Journals Administration Department
605 Third Avenue
New York, NY 10158
T: +1 212 850 6645
F: +1 212 850 6021
E: subinfo@wiley.com

Annual Subscription Rates 2001
Institutional Rate: UK £150
Personal Rate: UK £97
Student Rate: UK £70
Institutional Rate: US $225
Personal Rate: US $145
Student Rate: US $105

_AD_ is published bi-monthly.
Prices are for six issues and include postage and handling charges. Periodicals postage paid at Jamaica, NY 11431. Air freight and mailing in the USA by Publications Expediting Services Inc, 200 Meacham Avenue, Eimont, NY 11003

Single Issues UK: £19.99
Single Issues outside UK: US $32.50
Order two or more titles and postage is free. For orders of one title ad £2.00/US $5.00. To receive order by air please add £5.50/US $10.00

Postmaster
Send address changes to _AD_ c/o Expediting Services Inc, 200 Meacham Avenue, Long Island, NY 11003

Printed in Italy. All prices are subject to change without notice.
[ISSN: 0003-8504]

Cover image: Courtesy Lorenzo Romito, © Stalker

New Babylonians

Edited by Iain Borden and Sandy McCreery

Architectural Design +

Editorial

The situationist's vision of New Babylon is a shock. That is what Mark Wrigley surmises at the end of his description of Constant's presentation at the Stedelijk Museum in Amsterdam in 1960 (see p 11). There is little doubt that architectural thought and urban design is still reverberating with that shock. Though a utopian scheme, the New Babylon, which Constant Nieuwenhuys envisaged, was startlingly insightful in the contemporary tendencies it charted. Once the situationist vision had been unveiled, there could be no retreat from the broader acknowledgement of the massive transformations that were taking place in everyday life with the onset of mechanisation and an ever rapidly expanding population. The situationists were instrumental in exploding the 'modern' or post-enlightenment view of urban architecture as something that could be rationalised, organised and ultimately controlled. As Wrigley writes, Constant's urban vision was not that of 'a discrete object representing a huge project that may someday be built, we sense a complex, sensuous reality'. Instead of cities being determined by pre-planned structures, they are revealed as amorphous, human and ambient. Indeterminant sites of leisure and play, they are temporary, emergent and transitory.

In this issue of *Architectural Design*, Iain Borden and Sandy McCreery have done more than revisit the Situationist International – a postwar, French Marxist-revisionist group, starring Guy Debord and Constant, that debated the role of urbanism in a post-revolutionary future. They have brought together a diverse range of architects, thinkers and cultural commentators, who have sought to re-apply situationist thought in a contemporary context, thus extending and stretching current ideas on the city. As David Pinder writes on page 16, 'What is striking about the utopian spaces of New Babylon some three decades on is their provocative power, their disruptive edge and the critical challenge they pose to imagining the city otherwise.' Lorenzo Romito of Stalker rises to that critical challenge by proposing a means of redefining situationism in today's cultural and commercial context by reacting to it as a foil, much in the way that the situationists responded to their predecessors the surrealists. Carlos Villaneuva Brandt and his students produce two projects that envision a specific city, London, 'as otherwise'. Julia Chance's exploration of the Dutch practice West 8's work responds to Adriaan Geuze's comment that 'connections could be made' between his work and situationism. The architects and multi-media designers General Lighting & Power take on the Ludic challenge of situationism with a characteristically playful response that results in a series of jokes: 'What is the difference between a situationist and an Essex girl?' Play is also at the centre of Zoo's project for a recreation ground in inner city Glasgow. The inclusion of a critical essay by Karin Jaschke on the practices of Jerde Partnership International shifts the focus from the avant-garde to expansive, overtly commercial, retail-based developments. Colin Fournier drives situationism into cyberspace with a comparison between New Babylon and the Internet. The issue closes with a final worldwide *dérive* from Gil Doron, as he explores a universal architecture of transgression. Δ *Helen Castle*

Opposite
Adriaan Geuze and West 8,
Schouwburgplein, Rotterdam

5

Critique of Lines

For their introduction to the *New Babylonians*, Iain Borden and Sandy McCreery remain true to the spirit of the situationist project. Taking their title from Guy Debord's 1961 book, they rejoice in parodying and vandalising his original text.

We don't know what to say. So many things we wanted have not been attained; or have been attained only partially and not like we thought. What environments have we desired, or experienced, or only simulated? What true project has been lost?

The architectural spectacle has its rules, which enable one to produce satisfactory products. But dissatisfaction is the reality that must be taken as a point of departure. The function of architecture is to present an illusory, isolated coherence as a substitute for an urban complexity that is elsewhere. To demystify architecture it is necessary to dissolve what is called its function and meaning.

A well established rule is that anything in a building must hit like a hammer or else people will miss it. That may be true. But this sort of incomprehension is present everywhere in everyday encounters. Something must be specified, made clear, but there's not enough time and you are not sure that you have been understood. Before you have done or said what was necessary, you've already gone. Across the street. Overseas. There will never be another chance.

After all the dead time and lost moments there remain these endlessly traversed postcard landscapes; this distance organised between each and everyone. Childhood? It's right here; we have never grown out of it.

Our epoch accumulates powers and dreams of itself as being rational. But no one recognises these powers as their own. There is no entering into adulthood: only the possible transformation, someday, of this long restlessness into a routine somnolence. Because no one ceases to be held under guardianship. The problem is not that people live more or less poorly, but that they live in a way that is always out of their control.

At the same time, it is a world in which we have been taught change.

Nothing stops. It changes more every day; and we know that those who day after day produce change that acts against themselves can appropriate it for themselves.

The only adventure is to contest the totality, whose centre is this way of living, where we can test our strength but not use it. In reality no spatial adventure is truly our own. Buildings and public squares form part of the whole range of pre-existing narratives inscribed in the city; part of the whole spectacular sham of history.

Until the environment is collectively dominated, there will be no individuals – only spectres haunting the things that are anarchically presented to them by others. In chance situations we meet separated people moving randomly. Their divergent emotions neutralise each other and maintain their solid environment of boredom. As long as we are unable to make our own history, to freely create situations, the effort towards unity will introduce other separations. The quest for a central activity leads to the formation of new specialisations.

These New Babylonian projects are like signals emanating from a more intense life, a life that has not really been found. The search must go on.

The sectors of a city are, at a certain level, decipherable. But the personal meaning they have had for us is incommunicable, like all that clandestinity of private life for which we possess nothing but pitiful documents.

Official news is elsewhere. This society sends itself up with its historical image as a merely superficial and static geohistory of its rulers – those who incarnate the external fatality of what is done.

The sector of rulers is the very sector of the spectacle. Architecture suits them well. Moreover, architecture everywhere, and with everything it deals with, presents exemplary conduct modelled on the same old patterns.

All existing equilibrium, however, is brought back into question each time unknown people try to live differently. But this always happens far away. We learn of it through the Internet, magazines and broadcasts. We remain outside of it, confronted with just another spectacle. We are separated from it by our own non-intervention. It makes us disappointed in ourselves. At what moment was choice postponed? We have let things go.

We have let time slip away. We have lost what we should have defended. The hacienda has not been built.

Everything that concerns the sphere of loss – that is to say, the past time we have lost as well as disappearance, escape and, more generally, the flowing past of things and even what, in the prevalent and therefore most vulgar social sense of the use of time, is called wasted time – all this finds, in that strangely apt term 'outlaws', its meeting ground with the sphere of discovery, adventure, the avant-garde. This is the crossroads where we have found and lost ourselves.

This introduction, it must be admitted, is not clear. It is a typical and unfortunately sober offering, with its incomprehensible allusions, plagiarism and tiresome delivery. With its vain phrases which do not await response and its overbearing explanations. And its silences.

The poverty of means has to express plainly the scandalous poverty of the subject.

We have invented nothing. We adapt ourselves, with a few variations, into the network of possible courses. We get used to it, it seems.

On returning from a venture no one has the enthusiasm they had when they set out on it. Take our word for it, adventure is dead.

Who will resist? It is necessary to go beyond this partial defeat. Of course. And how to do it?

This is a book that interrupts itself and does not come to an end.

All conclusions remain to be drawn, everything has to be recalculated.

The problem continues to be posed, its expression is becoming more complicated. We have to resort to other measures.

Just as there was no profound reason to begin this introduction, so there is none for concluding it.

We have scarcely begun to make you understand that we don't intend to play the game. ∞

Stolen from Guy Debord's *Critique of Separation* (1961), and vandalised by Iain Borden and Sandy McCreery (2001).

NEW BABYLON NORD

The Great Urbanism
Game

The architectural historian Mark Wigley describes the moment in 1960 when the Dutch artist Constant Nieuwenhuys chose to reveal his vision of a 'New Babylon' to an audience at the Stedelijk Museum in Amsterdam. A powerful presentation of numerous images and plans accompanied by an ambient soundtrack, it delivered a startling and all-too-real picture of all-consuming urbanism.

20 December 1960. 8.15 pm. Amsterdam. A packed room in the Stedelijk Museum waits for the 40-year old artist Constant Nieuwenhuys. A slide projector and a large tape recorder sit behind the audience. Constant enters, stands by the machines, and delivers a half-hour statement on 'unitary urbanism'. The tone is militant.

Modern architects are negligent. They have systematically ignored the massive transformation of everyday life caused by the twin forces of mechanisation and population explosion. Their endless garden-city schemes desperately provide token fragments of 'pseudo-nature' to pacify ruthlessly exploited citizens. The modern city is a thinly disguised mechanism for extracting productivity from its inhabitants, a huge machine that destroys the very life it is meant to foster. Such exploitative machinery will continue to grow until a single vast urban structure occupies the whole surface of the earth. Nature has already been replaced. Technology has long been the new nature that must now be creatively transformed to support a new culture. The increasingly traumatised inhabitants have to take over the shaping of their own spaces to recover the pleasure of living. This reshaping will soon become their dominant activity when automation handles all forms of production. Leisure time will be the only time. Work gives way to an endless collective play in which all fantasies are acted out. The static constructions of architects and town planners are thrown away. Everybody becomes an architect, practising a never-ending, all-embracing 'unitary urbanism'. Nothing will be fixed. The new urbanism exists in time, it is the activation of the temporary, the emergent and the transitory, the changeable, the volatile, the variable, the immediately fulfilling and satisfying. An intimate bonding of desire and space will produce a new kind of architecture for a new society.

The lecturer announces that he has a particular vision of his restless architecture, an 'imaginary' project called 'New Babylon' which he will reveal later. Meanwhile, the audience hears an analysis of the psychological impact of urban environments. People are profoundly influenced by the structures they inhabit. Their lives are conditioned by the unique atmosphere of each space. To neglect the nuances of ambience is to neglect people.

As the world turns into a single vast city and an exploding, increasingly mobile population has less and less room to move, a new relationship between space and psychology is needed: 'What we lose in geometrical space we must recover in the form of psychological space.' A special form of research needs to be deployed, a 'psychogeography' of the unconscious influences of the urban atmosphere. Atmosphere is to become an 'artistic medium' with which to collectively reconstruct social space. The psychological quality of every point in the urban structure will be continuously modified to intensify the experience of the people moving through it. All forms of mobility will be fostered. The structure will itself be mobile and lack a clear identity.

Some details of the project start to emerge. New Babylon is to be a covered city, suspended high above the ground on huge columns. All automobile traffic is isolated on the ground plane, beneath which trains and fully automated factories are buried. Enormous multilevel structures, 5 to 10 hectares in area, are strung together in a chain that spreads across the landscape. This 'endless expanse' of interior space is artificially lit and air-conditioned. Its inhabitants are given access to powerful, ambience-creating resources to construct their own spaces whenever and wherever they desire. The qualities of each space can be adjusted. Light, acoustics, colour, ventilation, texture, temperature and moisture are infinitely variable. Movable floors, partitions, ramps, ladders, bridges and stairs are used to construct 'veritable labyrinths of the most heterogeneous forms' in which desires continuously interact. Sensuous space may rise from action but also generate it: 'New Babylonians play a game of their own designing, against a backdrop they have designed themselves.'

The lights go out. The room is filled with a strange unintelligible noise. A huge architectural plan is projected on the wall. It shows a network of long, thin, rectangular structures zigzagging like dominoes across an orange landscape covered with amorphous red and green blotches. The network sits on top of an even more intricate web of black lines that rush in every direction with what seem to be high-speed streamlined curves. Railway tracks pass more soberly across them. Intersections multiply. Everything is interconnected. The overlapping webs disappear off the edges of the plan and the ends of the webs enter from the sides. The already huge megastructure is apparently just part of a vast system. It is lightly subdivided into countless squarish spaces that are empty except for a small red rectangle in each that always occupies a different position. Larger black shapes pass through the divisions between these spaces and sometimes overtake a whole section of the structure. Some spaces are numbered sequentially. Others are crosshatched, or filled with parallel lines, or have mysterious arrows radiating from their corners. On the left of the plan, a thin line wanders in a serpentine trajectory across

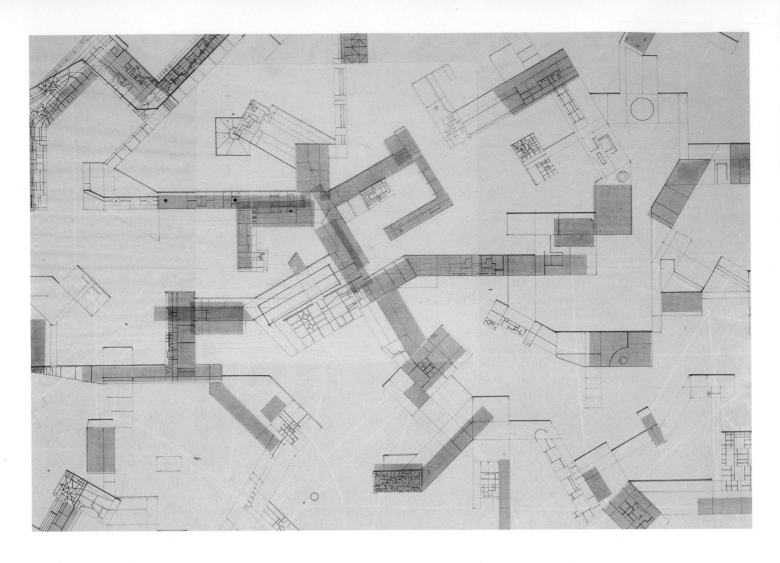

the divisions between spaces. At the bottom, a very thick line passes up through the structure, crossing each space in turn as it zigzags all the way to the centre of the plan – a path to the heart of the labyrinth.

The qualities of the particular spaces remain unclear; only a general sense of diversity within a more or less regular but labyrinthine system can be perceived. The image is there for just a second. Another plan appears. It is obviously the same project – a closer view. Rough edges have given way to precisely measured lines. The spaces are more complex, ranging in their organisation from completely open to being densely packed with labyrinths. Even the type of labyrinth varies. Eccentric paths could traverse this veritable catalogue of spatial types to pass between any two points in the megastructure without going outside it. If anything, the labyrinthine quality is accentuated by a sense of transparency on the plan. All levels are compacted on to a single surface. The high-speed lines are visible as they pass under the structure, and at the densest intersection a square of translucent yellow paper has been superimposed as if to define some vague sense of focus.

This layout now reappears as a bird's eye photograph of a model, an even closer view. The model still looks like a plan because it is built out of transparent layers of Plexiglass. The subdivisions etched in thin lines on each layer produce an extremely dense overlapping pattern, itself overlaid on the web of high-speed lines.

A few opaque pieces of white and black Plexiglass stand out, but only a faint shadow hints at the three-dimensional shape revealed in the next slide. Moving in closer, at an angle, the camera discovers that the high-speed lines race across a smooth plane while the megastructure floats above it. A single continuous structure weaves itself over an immaculate surface. Its section constantly changes. Some parts are made of a single thick slab of Plexiglass while others are made of two, three or four layers. The layers float high above the terrain or are unexpectedly cut away to expose the next level. Nails passing through them are arranged in a structural grid that supports the project, while a smaller grid of tiny holes appears to provide the local support for endless variations in the plan. The camera drops lower still. It reaches ground level and looks across the smooth terrain towards the building. The floating horizontal megastructure catches the light and stretches as far as the eye can see.

The camera descends upon another model. The sound of an aeroplane accompanies the descent and another set of sounds fills the room as we land on the roof deck. Each image-shift is synchronised with an acoustic shift although the sounds remain largely unintelligible. We head into the interior spaces that float between the roof deck covered with helicopters and the ground plane littered with cars. Only a few human figures are visible, perched on the edge of a vast space, but the soundtrack fills the auditorium with a metropolitan jumble of voices, traffic noises, machines, animals and strange music. We hear the sounds of a life that we cannot see, a life we are forced to imagine.

Our fantasies are made possible by sophisticated models that have been photographed in a way that conceals the fact that they are models. We never see their edges. Rather than viewing a small discreet object representing a huge project that may someday be built, we sense a complex, sensuous, built reality. Other spaces often appear in the background. The models have been placed side by side and coloured sand is sprinkled over the gaps between their bases to suggest the sense of a single coherent ensemble. We look into an endless world made up of tightly interconnected but heterogeneous spaces. Coloured backgrounds and precise lighting enhance the realism. Images move quickly. Time only for an impression.

The images follow a pattern. Models of large parts of the structure give way to detailed models of smaller parts; each is progressively explored from the widest distant angle down to the smallest interior space. We steadily advance into the new world. Any disruption of this relentless zoom is accompanied by a surprising sound. The precise layout of each level gradually becomes evident. The floating transparent layers carry a delicate tracery of some kind of embedded technical system and the divisions between spaces are formed by folded metal sheets, perforated metal screens, cut outs in the floor, changes in lighting and so on. Strange machinery sprouts from the ground plane or hangs from the ceiling. Each 'sector', as Constant calls them, seems to rest on a different kind of support. Some have an array of diverse supports. Huge, open frameworks sit on a small number of points. Dense layers are propped up on a massive translucent sandwich. Spider webs of steel are suspended from a tall cylinder. Transparent shells hover over the ground on vast columns, like recently landed spaceships. Intricate assemblages of platforms and volumes hang from each support.

Sometimes the ground below is an immaculately smooth white surface, like a salt lake ready for high-speed tests. Elsewhere, it is rough – like a moonscape – or covered with huge concrete labyrinths, strange marks and coloured patches. The immaculate metalwork and transparent surfaces of the structure contrast with the tortured landscape below. Other parts of the terrain are domesticated with abstractly coloured volumes, curved metal railings, strange dotted lines, densely packed nails or an artificial forest made of a network of wires strung between delicate columns. High overhead, metal sheets fold their way across a space or form vast surfaces. Translucent planes of different colours are suspended in intricate webs of metal. The overall lighting changes from red to blue to yellow to orange. Coloured shadows are cast in every direction, producing blurry zones of imagined activity. The effect is at once precise and indeterminate. It is as if the very realism of the image frees the imagination. The sheer number of images collaborates with the sounds to increase the sense of realism. A technological aesthetic acts as the prop for an intense fantasy about a new but unspecified life.

After more than 100 images have been shown, the last suddenly evaporates and the lights return. The audience is still blinking when a single cheer of 'Bravo!' rings out. But in the extended discussion that follows, there are protests. New Babylon might be the liberating way of the future, or it might just as easily be a nightmarish High Tech pleasure prison. Either way, it is a shock. ⌀

Mark Wigley is an architectural historian and theorist. This text is from Mark Wigley (ed), *Constant's New Babylon: Hyper-architecture of Desire*, 010 Publishers (Rotterdam), 1998.

Opposite top
Groep Sectoren (Group of Sectors), 1959. Collotype and ink; 57 x 68 centimetres, Gemeentemuseum, The Hague.

Opposite bottom
Groep Sectoren (Group of Sectors), 1959. Plexiglas; 100 x 100 centimetres, Gemeentemuseum, The Hague.

New Babylon/An urbanism of the future

by Constant Nieuwenhuys

Since the beginning of this century there has been constant discussion about the creative faculties of the human race, and more than one *avante-garde* movement has declared itself in favour of a *poésie faite par tous*. The realization of such a mass-culture does obviously not depend on the intentions of artists only, and would demand thorough changes within society.

If this is so, we can begin to understand the critical situation the artists have come into since the industrial revolution.

The effects of machine-production are leading slowly to a reduction in human labour, and we can state already with certainty, that we will enter a new era, in which production-labour will be automatic. For the first time in history, mankind will be able to establish an affluent society in which nobody will have to waste his forces, and in which everybody will be able to use his entire energy for the development of his creative capacities.

We can already say that there is no repeatable action that theoretically cannot be done by machine. The only activity that will remain beyond automation is the unique act of the imagination by which a human being is distinguished. The only field of activity unaccessible for the computer is the unforeseeable creativity that makes man change the world and reshape it after his capricious needs.

There can be no doubt about the progressing of mankind towards this prospect. No force on earth can possibly prevent humanity from seizing the affluence of automatic production that will enable man to live a creative life instead of being merely an instrument of production.

The question is, how the free man of the future will use his unlimited energies. It is clear that no comparison can be made to the artist of the past or of the present. The *homo ludens* of the past, like Johan Huizinga described him, was a man in an exceptional situation, a man who escaped reality in substituting another dreamed 'reality' that should help him to forget the unsatisfying circumstances of his actual life. No real contact was possible between him and the others who could not follow him into his substitute-reality, being confined themselves in utilitarian lives. His thoughts and his morals had to be different from the normal, and even when society recognized him, he remained a lonely man, sometimes an outcast. The new *homo ludens* of the future on the contrary, will rather be the normal type of man. His life will consist in constructing the reality he wants, in creating the world he conceives freely, no longer bothered by the struggle for life. We will see that this means a complete revolution in the field of social behaviour. If man is no longer bound to production-labour, he also will no longer be forced to stick to a fixed place, to settle down. He will be able to circulate, to change his environment, to enlarge his area. His relationship to space will become as free as his relationship to time is already becoming now.

The *homo ludens* of the future society will not have to make art, for he can be creative in the practice of his daily life. He will be able to create life itself, and to shape it in correspondance with still unknown needs that will emerge only after he has obtained complete freedom.

Constant Nieuwenhuys is a Dutch painter and sculptor who now is almost exclusively involved in the creation of both the imagery and the supporting theory for a future urbanism. He now regards the individual art work as virtually obsolete. His thinking initially arose out of association with the situationist movement in Paris; his ideas have been influenced by Huizinga's book Homo Ludens. The adjacent text is an abridged version of a lecture given at the ICA, London.

1 & 2
Hypothetical plan and model of a section of New Babylon. Tracks indicate high-speed access routes; rectangle forms indicate multi-level deck structures, suspended above the earth in constant state of change

A detail view of suspended deck structures

New Babylon represents the environment the *homo ludens* is supposed to live in. For it should be clear that the functional cities that have been erected during the long period of history in which human lives were consecrated to utility, would by no means suit the totally different needs of the creative race of the *homo ludens*. The environment of the *homo ludens* has, first of all, to be flexible, changeable, assuring any movement, any change of place or change of mood, and any mode of behaviour.

It follows that New Babylon could not be a determined plan. On the contrary, every element would be left undetermined, mobile and flexible. For the people circulating in this enormous social space are expected to give the space its ever-changing shape; to divide it, to vary it, to create its different atmospheres, and to play their lives in a variety of surroundings.

There are two connected circumstances that have caused, especially in the past ten years, a critical situation in the highly industrialized countries. The first and most important is an increase of population that is leading to an almost complete urbanization of the landscape, destroying the land that originally was used in common. The other circumstance, related to this, is the growing importance of mechanical traffic that enlarges enormously the living space of each individual. These developments represent a new social situation no one can deny. The facts are simply there as a reality, and we have to deal with them. But we cannot allow traffic to destroy the social space of the cities, like it is doing now, and we cannot let the population growth be responsible for changing all landscape into one uninterrupted townscape, boring and dead, without any possibility for creating a more interesting way of living.

Every plan for the future that is as free as the New Babylon project, has to solve the problems that are posed by these circumstances, and any failure in solving them may be considered as an attack against the freedom of life. The urbanization consists of a coherent system of covered unities that I call sectors, and in between remain extensive open green spaces where nobody lives and where no buildings are to be found. This network-like system is unlimited, and could, theoretically, cover the entire surface of the earth. Because of the intensified use that is made of space, this means that the field of activity of each individual has practically no limits.

The sector itself—whose dimensions are much bigger than those of any present building—is a spatial system of levels, that leave the ground-level free for an intensive fast traffic. On top of it there may be airports or heliports, to assure the quick passage to sector-groups in other parts of the world.

The sector-floors are primarily empty. They represent a sort of extension of the earth-surface, a new skin that covers the earth and multiplies its living space.

The unfunctional character of this playground-like construction makes any logical division of the inner spaces senseless. We rather should think of a quite chaotic arrangement of small and bigger spaces that are constantly mounted and dismounted by means of standardized mobile construction-elements, like walls, floors and staircases. Thus the social space can be adapted to the ever-changing needs of an ever-changing population that is passing the sector system.

continued overleaf

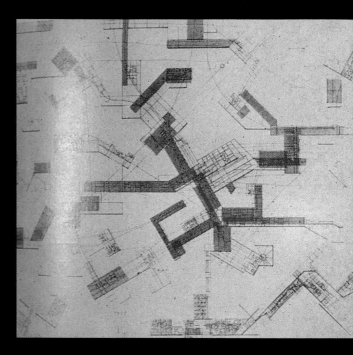

New Babylon:

An Urbanism of the Future

In June 1964 *Architectural Design* published this article by Constant, abridged from a lecture given at the ICA in London. In the four years since his presentation at the Stedelijk Museum in Amsterdam, so evocatively described by Mark Wigley in his previous article, Constant's ideas had notably shifted. He was expressing a new preoccupation with the importance of play in culture, as espoused by the Dutch Historian Johan Huizinga in his book *Homo Ludens*.

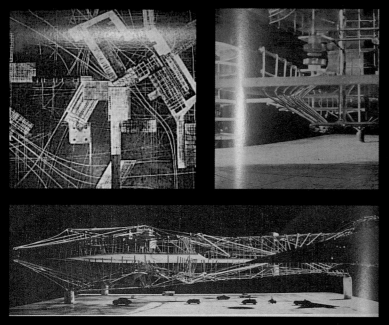

Since the beginning of the 20th century there has been constant discussion about the creative faculties of the human race, and more than one avant-garde movement has declared itself in favour of a *poésie faite par tous*. The realisation of such a mass culture obviously does not depend on the intentions of artists alone and would demand thorough changes within society. If this is so, we can begin to understand the critical situation artists have faced since the Industrial Revolution.

The effects of machine production are leading slowly to a reduction in human labour, and we can already state with certainty that we will enter a new era in which production-labour will be automatic. For the first time in history, mankind will be able to establish an affluent society in which no one will have to waste their energy, and in which everyone will be able to use it solely for the development of their creative capacities.

We can already say that in theory there is no repeatable action that cannot be done by a machine. The only activity that will remain beyond automation is the unique act of the imagination that distinguishes a human being from an automaton. The only field of activity the computer cannot access is the unforeseeable creativity that makes men and women change the world and reshape it after their capricious needs.

There can be no doubt that mankind is progressing towards this prospect. No force on earth can possibly prevent people seizing the affluence, created by automatic production, that will enable them to live creative lives instead of being merely instruments of production.

The question is how the free men and women of the future will use their unlimited energies. It is clear that no comparison can be made to artists of the past or present. The *Homo ludens* of the past, as Johan Huizinga described him, was a man in an exceptional situation, a man who escaped reality by substituting another dreamt 'reality' that would help him to forget the unsatisfying circumstances of his actual life. No real contact was possible between him and others who, being confined themselves in utilitarian lives, could not follow him into his substitute reality. His thoughts and morals had to be different from the normal, and even when society recognised him, he remained lonely, sometimes an outcast. The *Homo ludens* of the future, on the contrary, will be the normal type of human being. His life will consist of constructing the reality he wants, in creating the world he conceives freely, no longer bothered by the struggle for life. We will see that this means a complete revolution in the field of social behaviour. If someone is no longer bound to production-labour, they will no longer be forced to stay in a fixed place, to settle down. They will be able to circulate, to change their environment, enlarge their area. Their relationship to space will become as free as their relationship to time is already becoming.

The *Homo ludens* of the future society will not have to make art, for he will be able to be creative in the practice of his daily life. He will be able to create life itself and shape it to correspond with still unknown needs that will emerge only after he has obtained complete freedom.

New Babylon represents the environment *Homo ludens* is supposed to live in. For it should be clear that the functional cities erected during the long period of history in which human lives were dedicated to utility will by no means suit the totally different needs of the

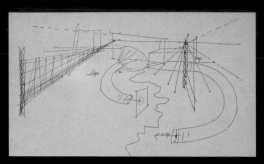

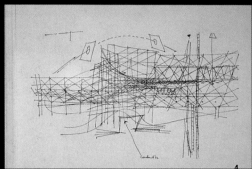

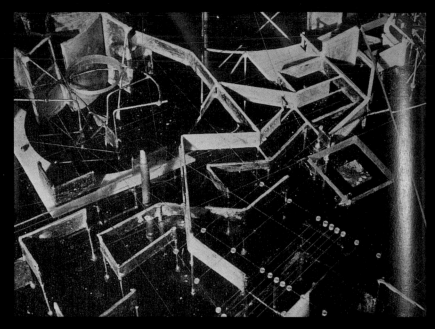

creative *Homo ludens*. The environment must, first of all, be flexible, changeable, open to any movement, change of place or mood, and any mode of behaviour.

It follows that New Babylon could not be structured to a determined plan. On the contrary, every element would be left undetermined, mobile and flexible. For the people circulating in this enormous social space are expected to give it its ever-changing shape; to divide it, to vary it, to create its different atmospheres and to play out their lives in a variety of surroundings.

Two connected circumstances have caused a critical situation in highly industrialised countries, especially in the past 10 years. The first and most important is an increase in population that is leading to the almost complete urbanisation of the landscape, destroying what was originally common land. The second, related to this, is the growing importance of mechanical traffic, which enormously enlarges the living space of each individual. No one can deny that these developments represent a new social situation. The facts are simply there as a reality, and we have to deal with them. But we cannot allow traffic to destroy the social space of cities, as it is doing now, and we cannot let population growth be responsible for changing all landscape into one uninterrupted townscape, boring and dead, that provides no possibility of creating a more interesting way of living.

Every plan for a future that is as free as the New Babylon project has to solve the problems posed by these circumstances, and any failure in solving them may be considered to be an attack on the freedom of life. In New Babylon, the urbanisation consists of a coherent system of

covered unities that I call sectors, and in between these there are extensive open green spaces where nobody lives and where no buildings are to be found. This network-like system is unlimited and could, theoretically, cover the entire surface of the earth. Because of the intensified use that is made of space, each individual's field of activity has practically no limits.

The sector itself – the dimensions of which are much bigger than those of any present building – is a spatial system of levels that leaves the ground level free for intensive fast traffic. On top of this structure there may be airports or heliports to ensure quick passage to sector-groups in other parts of the world. The sector floors are primarily empty. They represent a sort of extension of the earth's surface, a new skin that covers it and multiplies its living space.

The unfunctional character of this playground-like construction makes any logical division of the inner spaces senseless. We should rather think of a quite chaotic arrangement of small and bigger spaces that are constantly assembled and disassembled by means of standardised mobile construction elements like walls, floors and staircases. Thus the social space can be adapted to the ever-changing needs of an ever-changing population as it passes through the sector system.

There would be no question of any fixed life-pattern, for life itself would be a creative material. The unfunctional and fantastic way of living would demand rapid passage from one place to another, from sector to sector, and life in New Babylon would be essentially nomadic; people would constantly be travelling. There would be no need for them to return to their point of departure and this would in any case be transformed. Therefore, each sector would contain private rooms (a hotel) where people would spend the night or rest for a while. ⌀

Above left: top and bottom
Two sketches for New Babylon by Constant, dated 1961 and 1962. These give some indication of the constant movement-state envisaged.

Above right
The high level of a typical structure showing its surface divided by ever-changing mobile elements. The lines indicate past trajectories of movements or ones that are actually taking place. All Constant's models are made from metal and coloured elements of Perspex.

Utopian
Transfiguration:
The Other Spaces of New Babylon

David Pinder explores the unique poignancy of Constant's vision of New Babylon, with its dynamic and disconcerting spaces. This is at a time when the idealism of other earlier utopian fantasies tends to elude us.

New Babylon Today

What is to be made of the utopianism of Constant's New Babylon today? How to approach his visions of 'another city and another urban life' as evoked in the array of models, maps, plans, paintings, drawings, writings, lectures and visual presentations that occupied the artist for around 20 years? How to do so, more specifically, at a time when many critics have been content to announce the 'end of utopia', to wave goodbye to dreams of radically transforming the spaces and societies within which we live?

Yet it is not nostalgia for a more optimistic age that draws one back to these projects; nor is it the prospect of consolation, the chance to revive spirits wearied by contemporary political cynicism by dipping into warming streams of earlier visionary proposals now safely ensconced in museums. New Babylon's dreams of the liberation of humanity and the continual free creation of space, enabled by the automation of productive labour and the collective socialisation of land, certainly need to be understood in their historical context. This includes not only the architectural and design debates that have commanded the attention of much of the recent literature on the subject, but also other strands

Issues of space are frequently privileged, on the assumption that if these are sorted out social matters will follow.

of utopian thinking and activism that, during the 1960s, looked towards the possibilities of a creative society of abundance. Most particularly, these involved critical theorists and radical leftists who sought to realise a revolutionary transformation of society through a transition from what Marx called the 'realm of necessity' to the 'realm of freedom'. However, what is striking about the utopian spaces of New Babylon some three decades on is their provocative power, their disruptive edge and the critical challenge they pose to imagining the city otherwise. In returning to them today, one is confronted by still urgent questions about how to think about and encourage the creation of another space, an emancipatory geography, through radical social and spatial change.

Paradise on Earth

Utopian visions of the city are traditionally based on ordered spatial forms. These provide the settings for ordered, harmonious societies in which the ills of the present day are banished to another space or time. Issues of space are frequently privileged, on the assumption that if these are sorted out, social matters will follow. New Babylon sits critically within such a utopian tradition. Constant certainly referenced other classic utopian visions of cities, and kept in his archive depictions of Campanella's 'city of the sun', Victor Considérant's drawing of Fourier's phalanstery and Ebenezer Howard's diagrams of the garden city among other images. He also at times toyed with strategies familiar from utopian literature, such as constructing an 'atlas' of New Babylon, and at one stage proposed a tour guide that would lead readers on an imaginative journey through different sectors of his schemes. But he subverts many aspects of the lineage of which the earlier utopias are part.

The name 'New Babylon' itself carries a sense of challenging conventional expectations. The title came out of discussions with the situationist Guy Debord in 1959, when Constant was a member of the Situationist International. In dialogue with the poet Simon Vinkenoog for a programme on Dutch television, Constant commented on some of the complex associations of the title. In particular he referred to Babylon's reputation as 'the city of sin', compared to Zion as 'the city of God' where 'prayer and work' are the highest goals. He discussed how Babylon has traditionally been depicted as encircled by a snake, which appears to offer it as a forbidden fruit. But he argued that history reveals it to have been a cultural centre, a cosmopolitan city of freedom where the first civil law was written, as well as a place famous for its terraces and hanging gardens. He asserted that the possibilities of the present era provide an opportunity to reclaim the name of Babylon as an image of freedom and luxury. Now, 2,500 years later, 'we can play with a thought of a paradise on earth, a new Babylon, the city of the automatised age.'

Constant was in fact uneasy with the description of New Babylon as 'utopian'. He stressed that the changes he was envisaging were within reach, that they were based on possibilities being opened up by new technical, economic and social conditions. While acknowledging its utopian aspects, he therefore at times preferred to call it a 'realistic project'. In part, this was to be deliberately provocative as he sought to shake up current approaches to urbanism. But it also reflected important facets of the situationists' early discussions of 'unitary urbanism' from which New Babylon initially emerged.

For the situationists, the aim of unitary urbanism was not to build fantastic dream worlds disconnected

from reality. Rather, it was to change reality and to intervene in the production of space through the conscious and collective creation of an environment based on the possibilities inherent within the present. Unitary urbanism was meant to be visionary, in that it 'envisages a terrain of experience for the social space of the cities of the future'; but it was also bound up with current experimentation and political struggle, directed towards developing a ludic and agonistic engagement with existing cities in the belief that it 'has already begun the moment it appears as a programme of research and development.' Although Constant resigned from the Situationist International a year after this collective statement on unitary urbanism was published, an avant-garde commitment to bringing together artistic and political practices to transform everyday space remained important to his work on New Babylon.

Critical Provocations
Alongside the images of utopian cities in Constant's archives can be found other photographs that are indicative of his critical intentions. A mass of cars is seen from the air, sprawling across an unidentified area of land. A magazine cutting shows a baseball stadium in Milwaukee, again viewed from the air. The stadium is packed with thousands of spectators, who are in turn surrounded by their cars. The image was reproduced in the situationists' journal with the caption: 'Social space of leisure consumption'. A further aerial perspective shows the centre of Amsterdam, in a photograph that had featured in the previous issue of the

Unitary urbanism was conceived as an attempt to reclaim social space, to construct cities for pleasure, adventure and a creative unfolding of life.

journal with the caption 'Experimental zone for the dérive'. Instead of being given over to the circulation of traffic or to commercialised leisure activities, urban space is here invested with the contrasting promise of future games and wanderings, in which the city's potential will be explored critically, and its terrain approached in terms of play, desire and collective creativity.

As these images suggest, Constant's work on New Babylon involved criticism of present urban spaces, and especially of the reconstitution of cities in postwar Europe according to the interests of capital and bureaucratic states. Like his situationist associates, he attacked the 'dismal and sterile ambience in our surroundings' that prevented the kind of creative urban behaviour and encounters they were seeking. He compared the new towns under construction in many European countries to 'cemeteries of reinforced concrete ... in which the great masses of the population are condemned to die of boredom.' He was also sharply critical of modernist planning schemes influenced by earlier utopian proposals such as those of Ebenezer Howard or the Congrès Internationaux d'Architecture Moderne (CIAM), and especially the work of Le Corbusier, blaming them for carving up social space in the city. Unitary urbanism was conceived as an attempt to reclaim social space, to construct cities for pleasure, adventure and a creative unfolding of life.

When reproductions of Constant's initial models first appeared in situationist publications they were presented with this critical and interventionist spirit in mind. A short unsigned article in *Potlatch*, which featured a photograph of Constant's 'Ambiance of a future city', and which referred to an exhibition he held at the Stedelijk Museum in Amsterdam in May 1959, argued that his models went beyond 'merchandise-objects', whose role was to be only looked at, and instead were 'project-objects, whose complex appreciation calls for some sort of action, an action on a higher level having to do with the totality of life.' As the models and materials for New Babylon expanded dramatically over subsequent years, their collective manifestation as a project – and especially one aimed at provocation – developed.

New Babylon was never meant to be an urban plan or a formal vision of built form. Instead, it was a means of instigating a new understanding of urban space and of encouraging, as well as imagining, a medium for a new approach to urban living. Constant described it as an 'experimental thought and play model for the establishment of principles for a new and different culture.' His artworks and presentations serve to unsettle, disturb and disorient assumptions about urban life and form. From the radicalism of his theoretical pronouncements to the clashing and swirling lines of his drawings, the creative energy and festivity of some of his paintings and the labyrinthine structures and sector models shown in slides and films during lectures accompanied by soundtracks (as is so vividly described by Mark Wigley in this volume) – his emphasis is on provoking responses, on challenging imaginations. The passivity associated with the urban spectacle, with its basis in the principle of nonintervention, is to be undermined and the dormant powers of creativity awakened. Meanwhile a realm that is necessarily unknown is to be approached.

Constant seeks to open ways of envisaging the 'other city' and 'other life' of New Babylon through evoking alternative atmospheres and realities. Openness, flexibility and indeterminacy are therefore key themes in his works. The process has to be experimental and vague, for the needs and desires that would give shape to the city cannot be known in advance of the qualitative break or emancipation that allows them to emerge, that transfiguration that is characteristic of the utopian moment of critique. At the same time, however, this is a source of tension, apparent in Constant's outlines for New Babylon. He provides images and representations as part of a 'play model',

---

Utopian dreams about cities are often dismissed as irrelevant fantasies or compensatory distractions, or for being necessarily authoritarian with their fixed plans and proposals for spatial forms.

---

materialising understandings of space and engaging with an imaginary environment. But he also recognises the difficulties of doing so from within the restrictive conditions of the present, as well as the constraining implications of fixing depictions of a supposedly dynamic space in this way. Hence the manner in which he undercuts stasis, shifts perspectives, emphasises change and movement while all the same working with particular spatialisations. Hence, too, his ultimate and oft-repeated reminder: that the production of the spaces of New Babylon will be the work of the New Babylonians themselves,

Spaces of Desire
The utopianism of New Babylon is therefore not directed towards presenting an ordered vision of the city. It does not present a formal plan or blueprint to be realised in the future, nor a vision based on a harmonious arrangement of space and society. As a utopian space, it can be understood as a repository of desire for a

different and better future. But far from being a vision that could be construed as consoling or compensatory, it seeks to disturb, to displace assumptions and to open up perspectives on how other spaces and other modes of living might be produced. The emphasis is on the possible, on what could be, and on realising desires through processes of social and spatial change. The sense of dissonance, conflict and contradiction that remains within it is an intrinsic part of the project, a mark of more general tensions within utopian imaginations that seek to take the transformation of society and space seriously.

If this suggests a notion of utopianism that is at odds with those often associated with currents of utopian urbanism, with their ordered and harmonious arrangements of space, then it connects with the approaches adopted by a number of critics who have rethought the place of utopia within critical thought. A notable example is the Marxist philosopher Henri Lefebvre, who often visited Constant in Amsterdam during the 1960s and spoke favourably of the latter's work on New Babylon, seeing it as connecting with his own developing concerns with spatial politics and asserting the 'right to the city'. For both of them, space is understood in social and political terms, as something that is produced and contested. Utopian spaces are themselves thought of as social; not as fixed goals or containers for society but as dynamic and continually in process through the struggle for change.

It is valuable to remember such perspectives in the present period when there is so much talk of the end of utopia. Utopian dreams about cities are often dismissed as irrelevant fantasies or compensatory distractions, or for being necessarily authoritarian with their fixed plans and proposals for spatial forms. But it is important to assert that utopianism need not be about proposing static solutions or blueprints for the future, that it can be open, dynamic and provocative. There is indeed a need for projects that seek to prise open understandings of the present, that offer glimpses of other possibilities and that maintain a creative game with current conditions in order to figure alternatives. New Babylon is imbued with a sense of what the philosopher Ernst Bloch called the 'not yet'. It insists on what is missing, absent, still not in the present, and at the same time it looks towards what is a real possibility, what is 'not yet' in the sense of 'still to come'. This double consciousness needs to be at the heart of contemporary attempts to build on New Babylon's radical legacy. ◬

David Pinder lectures in human geography. The themes of this essay are developed in his *Visions of the City: Utopianism, Power and Politics in Twentieth-Century Urbanism*, Edinburgh University Press (Edinburgh), forthcoming.

Notes
1. 'Met Simon Vinkenoog naar het New Babylon van Constant'; transcript from 'Atelierbezoek: Simon Vinkenoog bezoekt Constant', broadcast on vpro-Television, 4 February 1962.
2. Constant, 'Unitair urbanisme'; manuscript of lecture at the Stedelijk Museum, Amsterdam, 20 December 1960; translated by Robyn de Jong-Dalziel as 'Unitary urbanism' in Mark Wigley (ed), *Constant's New Babylon: The Hyper-Architecture of Desire*, 010 Publishers (Rotterdam), 1998, p 132.
3. 'L'urbanisme unitaire à la fin des années 50', *Internationale Situationniste*, 3 (December 1959) pp 11–16; translated by Paul Hammond as 'Unitary urbanism at the end of the 1950s' in Libero Andreotti and Xavier Costa (eds), *Theory of the Dérive and Other Situationist Writings on the City*, Museu d'Art Contemporani/actar (Barcelona), 1996, pp 83–4. Emphasis in the original.
4. *Internationale situationniste*, 4 (June 1960), p 4.
5. *Internationale situationniste*, 3 (December 1959), p 15.
6. Constant, 'Une autre ville pour une autre vie', *Internationale Situationniste*, 3 (December 1959), pp 37–40; translated by Paul Hammond as 'Another city for another life' in Andreotti and Costa, op cit, p 92.
7. 'Premières maquettes pour l'urbanisme nouveau', *Potlatch*, 30, new series No 1 (15 July 1959); translated by Gerardo Denìs as 'Preliminary models for a new urbanism' in Andreotti and Costa, op cit, p 62.
8. Constant, 'New Babylon' in *Constant Amsterdam*, Städtische Kunstgalerie (Bochum), March/April 1961, no pagination; partially translated in Ulrich Conrads (ed), *Programmes and Manifestoes on 20th-Century Architecture*, MIT Press (Cambridge, Mass), p 177. Emphasis in the original.
9. See Seyla Benhabib, *Critique, Norm and Utopia: A Study in the Foundations of Critical Theory*, Columbia University Press (New York), 1986.
10. Constant, 'Autodialogue on New Babylon', *Opus International*, 27 (September 1971), p 80.

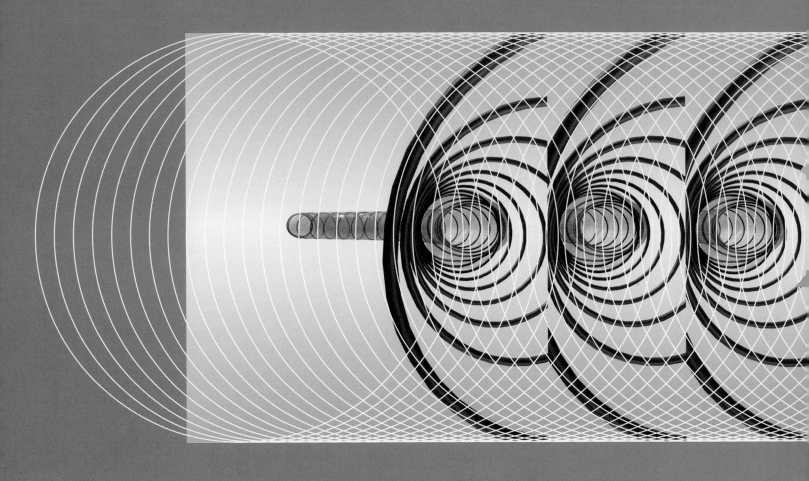

The Surreal Foil

For the Situationist International, the success of the Surrealist movement presented a departure point or foil for the development of their ideas. Here Lorenzo Romito of the interdisciplinary Rome-based practice Stalker explains how the current popularity of situationist thinking among the avant-garde has provided a similar counterpoint for them.

The very success of Surrealism has a lot to do with the fact that the most modern side of this society's ideology has renounced a strict hierarchy of factitious values and openly uses the irrational, including vestiges of Surrealism.[1]
Guy Debord

From their inception the Situationist International offered a strenuous critique of Surrealism: '... In a world that had not changed, Surrealism became a success.' The same success is now enjoyed by situationism: repeatedly evoked by the radical avant-garde both in art and architecture it is getting renewed attention. Today one could perhaps apply to the situationists the same critique that they applied to the surrealists. The distance that existed between Surrealism and the modern world has now decreased and new manifestations in progressive disciplines actually assume a Surrealist appearance. However, the reality behind this evolution is that, since no revolution took place, what constituted an edge of freedom for the surrealists has been revarnished and co-opted by the same repressive world they fought against.

By which I mean that the practice of the dérive and the construction of situations today can be exploited by the ideology of society, in the same way that Surrealist practices such as automatic writing, and collective games based on it, were exploited at the end of the 1950s.

The present world of communications, synthesis of information languages, propaganda and art has broken free from the television cage-box that flattened it into two dimensions, to invade space, time and collective behaviours. It makes use of the devices proposed by the situationists, though in an adulterated form – devices that are accepted and promoted by those who venture along the road of radical research today. Without suggesting that situationist practices are not up-to-date and necessary, I point out the danger that resides in the aestheticisation and social irrelevance of such practices and their mystifying, pervasive and totalising use at the hands of the society of the spectacle. As the situationists put it, the impotence of cultural creation preserves the actuality of Surrealism and fosters many of its degraded repetitions.

The gap between the situationists and the society of the spectacle is getting narrower and more blurred by the day, the result of the development of spectacular practices made possible by an exploitative, eviscerated and sterilised appropriation of situationist practices. This means that the society of the spectacle has somehow started to speak in a situationist language, an instrumental use that ignores the revolutionary values that underpin situationism. On the other hand, Guy Debord himself warned us about the pervasiveness of the society of the spectacle: it can transform any revolutionary innovation into a tool and even the destruction of language can be sanctioned as a positive value. His lurid and prophetic critiques denounce the passivity of the spectator as the insurmountable limit to

the society of the spectacle. That is why the situationists proposed the construction of situations as their winning card, an effective weapon against the society of the spectacle. This is what I perceive to be utopian – a dream that, Debord would say, risks inducing sleep.

In fact, if in the 1950s the term 'spectacular' could suitably describe the pervasive penetration of capitalism into real life, and the fostering of sleeping masses who passively endured a spectacle administered by television, today we must reckon with a society of the spectacle that has outlived the disaggregation of these masses and addresses the single spectator. It shocks him and puts him into situations that can be controlled – endless pseudo-liberties which give the impression that he can choose and shape spectacular situations that instead have been prepackaged. In today's society of the spectacle and pseudo-situations, the spectator is no longer passive; he is actively involved in a collective pseudo-game. These considerations are not meant to be a criticism of situationism, rather an attempt to redefine the practice, which is one of extreme importance for any experimental research but needs to be updated in the light of more penetrating and effective forms of capitalist spectacularisation.

The lesson contemporary forms of experimentation must learn from situationism is not limited to situationist practices such as the construction of situations, the dérive and psychogeography. A major insight we owe to Debord is the awareness that the spectacle is the preservation of unconsciousness within changes in the conditions of our conscious existence, even when existence is attained through the realisation of pseudo-ludic pseudo-situations that actively involve the spectator, who thus becomes actor and pseudo-viveur.

I believe that we must be aware that today's radical research is born in a territory dominated by the spectacle, or in a periphery that can be spectacularised. This awareness is useful if we are to avoid delusions and detect mystifications. What we can do is take advantage of the elasticity of this spectacular language and create environments and experimental situations, initially ephemeral and informal, where solidarity and truly ludic behaviours can flourish – environments whose realisation brings the consciousness that the conditions of existence can be changed.

We must sail the waves of spectacular reality, aware that the winds may change direction and that only consciousness of our course will take us to new shores. In this navigation it is more important to recognise the direction taken by those who sail next to us than to be impressed by the profiles of their flashy boats or by some pirate's flag. What must be verified is the effectiveness of these experimental practices, rather than their allegiance to an experimental language that cannot, and should not, be codified. ⚲

Note
1. Guy Debord, 'Report on the Construction of Situations and on the International Situationist Tendency's Conditions of Organisation and Action' (originally presented at the July 1957 Cosio d'Arroscia, Italy, conference at which the Situationist International was founded). Excerpts published in Ken Knabb (ed), *Situationist International Anthology*, Bureau of Public Secrets (Berkeley, Ca), 1981, pp 17–25. Sentence quoted, p 20.

Transborderline:
A habitable cross border structure, supporting the free circulation of people

An impenetrable spiral of barbed wire has often been the only three-dimensional representation of a border. The Transborderline is a new kind of border. Though it maintains a spiral shape it has shed the barbed wire and widened its diameter, transforming it into a potentially ludic space.

Habitable as well as crossable, the Transborderline creates a new prototype for public space that replaces the old borders. It creates an ideal place for exchange and the meeting of diversity. It is an infrastructure that can provide both structure and freedom of passage. Traces of former passersby are deposited along the Transborderline. Strangers are welcomed and there are spaces for meetings and public confrontation – ludic spaces for all ages. It is a public space for the recognition of difference, in which it is possible to play with borders, their symbolic value and what the reality of them might be when they are impenetrable; it is a space that allows borders to be crossed and transcended without being wiped out.

The Transborderline has been installed by Stalker at different sites, exploring the potential of the structure as a ludic space for interaction and confrontation. In the Villa Medici and at the Campo Boario in Rome, it was given to researchers who wanted to experiment with its possible applications. In two contemporaneous exhibitions, the Venice Biennale 2000 and the Ljubljana Manifesta 3 in Slovenia, part of the Transborderline was installed along the border between Italy and Yugoslavia while other parts of the conceptually connected structure were placed in the two cities. The installation represented an imaginary infrastructure crossing the borders between East and West. In the heart of both Ljubljana and Venice thousands of footballs were exchanged, on which were written the names, stories and desires of people crossing the borders of Europe. The project was intended to contribute to confrontation and exchange with the 'other', and to the free circulation of people. △

Images at the Edge of the Built

In many ways the oversized advertising hoardings and large-size photographic images which now dominate city streets worldwide were anticipated by the situationists' idea of spectacle. Through Krzysztof Kiéslowski's film *Three Colours Red*, and his own photographs of New York City and Sydney, Charles Rice provides an alternative account of the city as a space of image perception. For, rather than alienation and distraction, he finds that these spatial fantasies effectively deliver identification with the distant and unattainable.

In Krzysztof Kiéslowski's 1994 film *Three Colours Red* the protagonist, Valentine, is photographed for an advertisement which is reproduced at a scale of 25 x 65 feet at a major intersection in Geneva. Within the film's image, she is produced as an image in the city. The story of the film is about the spatial and temporal relations between the characters. The relationship between Valentine and her near neighbour, Auguste, is marked by both closeness and distance in spatial terms. They live in close proximity, in similar first-floor apartments that are visible to each other and overlook the same cross-streets. As they emerge from their apartments as part of their daily lives, they appear to be circling each other, almost wilfully. Their habitual city space is shared, but they are distanced by the effect of habit that renders urban subjects anonymous.

But the image of Valentine unfurled in another part of Geneva arrests Auguste. He stops his car at a red light and sees it. He is momentarily absorbed by it, missing the change of lights from red to green. The image, a profile of Valentine against a billowing red background, is, bizarrely, advertising chewing gum. Some

form of proximity is finally enacted between Valentine and Auguste, but it is a proximity that takes place through an image.

But what, or whom, is Auguste seeing? I want to claim that he is seeing three things: an image at the edge of the built; an image of a face; and an image that is a reflection. These three perceptual moments sketch out a spatialised perception of images in the city.

In a kind of doubling of this cinematic example, images in New York and Sydney share something of the cinematic in their scale, ratio, framing, figural sharpness and, most significantly, for the way they engage with subjects who perceive them. Most often these images are advertisements, but in calling them cinematic I mean to introduce a new way of thinking about their place within the city: that they are not merely advertising signs, but rather have a particular affectivity that is spatialised. The short sequence from *Red*, demonstrates this affectivity of the image. Auguste is not given a product – chewing gum – 'to have', so much as the image of a subjectivity 'to be', as if the gum would provide the stuff of a new 'freshness of life', which is the advertising slogan. This *'fraîcheur de vivre'* extends Auguste's perception of the image with an identification, with the fantasy of 'living out' a subjectivity beyond the sign of consumption. As viewers

Opposite
ANZ Bank building, Sydney.

of the film, Kiéslowski gives us a particular and privileged knowledge of how this identification operates with images. He offers a kind of reflexive moment, for himself as film-maker and us as film-viewers.

In extending this theoretical apparatus borrowed from cinema, I want to describe the space of the city as both the space of image perception, and the space of this 'living out' of an identification. Auguste is brought close to an image, and what Kiéslowski deftly shows with this closeness is Auguste's distance from the person, Valentine, whose image is projected, no matter their spatial proximity. The viewer of the film is able to see the pathos of this situation, this tension between near and far, that offers an insight for the interaction between images and urban space. The inherited theoretical apparatus for the explication of modern urban experience privileges alienation, distraction, shock effects and the crowd as figures of experience. What certain images in the city provide is a reworking of these figures towards another account of urban affectivity: a closeness to those who remain distant, a closeness to an image that makes distant subjectivities attainable in identification and through a spatial fantasy.

At the Edge of the Built
Something of the displacing effects of the dérive is present in coming across such incongruous

objects as a book shelf in the middle of Sydney, a giftwrapped package in midtown Manhattan or a television screen at Times Square. These are images which create incongruous objects. Their scale is that of the building. Each replaces a building with an image and, in doing so, the images take on the object-character of their support. No frame is visible except for the city itself.

Advertising in these images functions in the mode of identification. The bookcase, for ANZ Bank, includes the discreetly placed slogan 'Grow with ANZ'. Judging by the carefully selected volumes, from literary classics to travel books to art and design titles, the bank appears to be lending not solely the monetary capital to buy a home, but the cultural capital that is required to inhabit it successfully. The Hermès gift box in Manhattan emphasises the successful display of giving, rather than the nature of the object given.

The cities are here turned into interiors. Objects proper to the home and its psychogeography emerge in the place of buildings. The subjective effect of this is to make urban experience a traversal of the subject's own interiority, an overscaled theatre where he or she can pace out this interior spatiality, walking through the city as if possessed of ANZ's cultural capital and the home that encases it, walking through the city and coming upon the perfect gift to give or be given; and being arrested by these images in the city with something of the stupor, the languidity involved in watching television. This imagistic dérive occurs not because of a reorganisation and a détournement of the

representations of cities, rather it occurs within the spatiality of urban experience. Yet this possibility occurs at the very edge of the built, when fabric is stretched taut over a building facade, or when it is given over to new screen technology or when the simple construction-hoarding presents a different sort of object to the city.

These images produced at the edge of the built are also caught up in particular temporal trajectories and modes of change. The speed of delivery of these images, tied to the trajectory of advertising, cuts across accepted notions of the temporality of change in cities. But the images also serve to rethink how temporality and change are thought about in cities. The construction-hoarding image exists because the time of construction is considered a kind of down time, after which a building will emerge, fully formed, into an environment that determines it as part of a much larger image of the solidity of civic or commercial space. This down time at the edge of the built is becoming more significant if one thinks of resultant building production as itself only contributing to a kind of image of the city.

Faces

For Auguste in *Red*, meeting or following the look of another face in the city produces arresting and disjunctive effects. The looks of such faces as the sunglassed train traveller on the New York end wall and Cathy Freeman in Sydney exist in two spaces. In the first, they look into the space of the image: not just the space depicted within it, but the space of the image's narrative. The train traveller inverts the city, folds it around his reclining position, as we become unsure exactly whose mind should be returned to the upright position. Cathy Freeman looks out on to the freeway flyover that becomes her running track. The look in these images opens up a space that, again, remakes the city's space, reorganising its elements to the scale and orientation of the figure depicted. But the residual space of the city – the space of the viewer arrested on the street by the image – also plays in this rearrangement. In this second space, the faces and figures on the hoardings look out of their images and down on to the city itself, often appearing to engage the viewer in direct eye contact. Thus, two spaces are gathered around these images: the ordinary, stable space of the solicitation of the viewer and the space the image remakes for the subject caught by its look. The face in the image becomes a sort of switch or relay between the possibility these two spaces open up for the subject. To become Cathy, to get closer to her image, the road in front must take on something of the running track she sees in the city.

Reflections

There are moments of confirmation for this fantasy of identification, this fantasy of taking another's place and having a space for this taking. Stopped in front of Lever House in New York, I am caught in my own photograph,

in my own attempt to make an image of experience, in my own attempt to experience the city as images and simultaneously to be in those images. As a confirmation of the ways in which cities can be remade in subjects' fantasies, the reflection of the self in the glass of the corporate foyer appears like a material manifestation of the possibility that cities are as much material fabrications as they are imaginative fantasies.

Something of a mediation between the image and the built is provided by Dan Graham at his installation on the roof of the Dia Art Foundation in New York. It is a simple two-volume enclosure, a cylinder enclosed within a perimeter square, the walls of each being transparent and semireflective. The specificity of its roof-top location gives it its imagistic nature. Manhattan sticks to its semi-reflective surfaces as a series of images. Its reflective qualities also project these images into the space of the city itself. The installation thus layers the city as images, and it is impossible not to see one's own reflection in these layers. It is impossible to extricate oneself from the city as images, even as one walks in the space of the glass corporate foyer Graham mimics.

This conjunction of the built and the image in the reflection offer both a confirmation and a caveat for the idea of building New Babylon. The confirmation comes with the notion that imagistic and imaginary effects are also material effects. To argue for the primacy of an experience of the built over an experience of the image ignores the fact that much of the power of the image comes from its association with imagination, from the remaking of a city in

a psychogeography that the city itself allows within its built spatiality. The caveat emerges with the realisation that the residual material spaces of cities do not have to be remade or ignored in the forging of new effects and new spaces in a New Babylon. The hubris associated with the projection of new forms also underestimates the subjective remaking of the city prompted by images at the edge of the built.

The Space of the Image

The experience of images as spatial phenomena is crucial to understanding the city traversed by subjects seeking other subjectivities. To displace the question of the image in cities, and in architectural discourse generally, on to the question of subjectivity seems at once more productive for engaging with issues of contemporary urban experience. The malleability of the city in a subject's lived-out, spatial fantasies posits as redundant arguments over the relative merit of images versus buildings in the city. What is and is not an image in these instances of fantasy ceases to become a determinable judgement. It is more pertinent to consider that images are spatialised when they are unfurled in cities.

What this consideration promotes is a new way of looking at both an experiential and a discursive level: a new way of looking both at images in cities, and at the situation of their spatial experience. This would recognise, firstly, that specific examples of the affectivity of space in contemporary cities can be discussed through the apparatus of the image; and, secondly, that this discussion of the affectivity of space gives an understanding of spatialisation to the apparatus of the image. ᗄ

Charles Rice is an architectural historian and theorist.

Opposite
Nike advertisement with Cathy Freeman, Sydney.

Above left
Reflections against Lever House, New York City.

Above right
Reflections in Dan Graham's two-way mirror cylinder inside cube, Dia Art Foundation, New York City.

Vauxhall X / City Hall

In a description of his own Vauxhall X project and Henrik Rothe and Ole Scheeren's design for City Hall, Carlos Villanueva Brandt sets up a comparison betweeen two juxtaposing proposals that explore different yet similar relationships between the social and physical dimensions of urban life in London.

Action, structure and image generate a dynamic dialogue between the user and the city which controls the perception of, and participation in, urban space. The city offers on the one hand an image of the ideal, and on the other a direct experience of the everyday. The ideal and everyday could be interpreted as being contradictory and incompatible, but are here understood to be equally crucial in setting up an appropriate urban condition. Similarly, issues related to social and physical structures, which are usually considered to be separate, are combined to generate an active urban space. Thus, the reality of the city becomes a combination of social and physical space. Through the reinterpretation of urban space and the implementation of fragmented physical structures, the Vauxhall X and City Hall projects allow for the introduction of social

networks that exploit the forces that control the city and encourage the simultaneous participation of institutions and individuals. Although they are two separate experiments which differ in detail, they have in common a shared goal: to define an architectural application that combines action with design in order to generate urban structures of continuity and transformation.

Vauxhall X, London
Carlos Villanueva Brandt

This theoretical project, which was commissioned as an installation for the 1997 Borderlines exhibition in Graz, Austria, establishes a quarter-mile circle of potential around Vauxhall Cross in London.

Various physical and social interventions are set up within this radius, establishing a series of separate territories. These combine to create a unified structure of public space. The separate but related territories are as follows: the river junction; billboard space; territories 1 (west), 2 (south), 3 (east), 4 (north); crossings 1, 2, 3, 4, 5 (from west to east); station junction; landscape junction.

Territories create different spaces which are implied by images. This sets up different relationships between image space and physical space within the territories. Hence the fragmented territories and images create a composite three-dimensional space.

Within the quarter-mile circle, the related territories form one continuous, asymmetric structure – an asymmetry governed by programme and/or use.

Point structures define the relationship between the institutions and the territories. Existing institutions (types) also influenced the design of the overall structure. Within the quarter-mile circle, existing types were recorded as follows, between 1 July and 31 August 1997:

Vauxhall Cross: 1 July to 31 August (photographs)
Metropolis (motorbikes): half day, 29 July (photographs)
NABC (clubs for young people): morning, 31 July (photographs) Government Office for London: morning,
1 August (meeting) Balloon Experience: 15 minutes, morning, 15 August (photographs)
Vauxhall Tavern (gay pub): Saturday night, 16 August (photographs)
Railtrack: morning, 21 August (telephone)
Hesters Butchers: afternoon, 26 August (photographs).

The proposed structure encourages a common public-space policy between the boroughs of Lambeth, Westminster and Wandsworth, who all function within the quarter-mile circle of potential, and thus defines an urban strategy for public space.

Opposite
The installation matrix aims to transport the urban condition of Vauxhall X to the exhibition space in Graz.

Above, top row: left to right
Times, Vauxhall Cross

Independence, Vauxhall Cross

Metropolis workshop

Spring Gardens,
Balloon Experience

Bottom row: left to right
Linda, Vauxhall Cross

Dave, butcher, at Hesters Butchers

NABC Club

Balloon Cross,
Balloon Experience

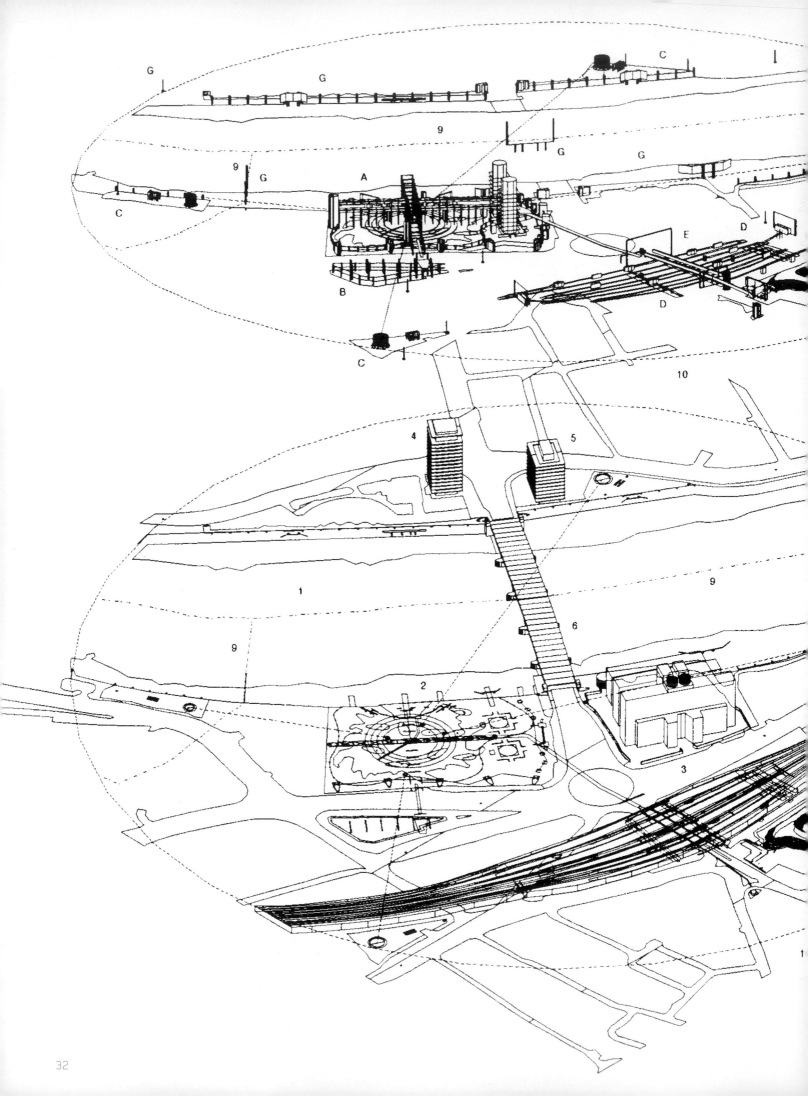

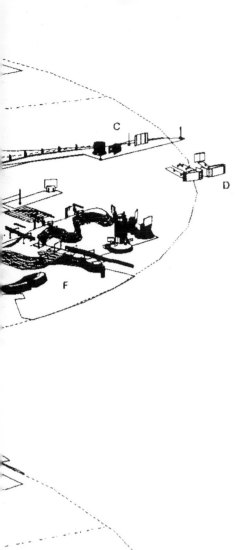

Site Elements
1 = Thames, 2 = Effra site, 3 = MI6, 4 = Previous British Gas tower, 5 = Government Office for London, 6 = Vauxhall Bridge, 7 = Vauxhall Station, 8 = Spring Gardens, 9 = Boundaries

Photograph Locations
10 = Vauxhall Cross, 11 = Metropolis, 12 = Balloon Experience, 13 = Vauxhall Tavern, 14 = nabc, 15 = Hesters Butchers

A = River junction. A social territory that links Vauxhall Cross to the city is created. It is to be used for social events and colonised by new and existing social institutions. The river junction becomes the fourth key structure adjacent to Vauxhall Bridge, which sets up physical, conceptual, programmatic and social links with the related territories of Vauxhall Cross.

B = Billboard space. A two-level structure within the territory is enclosed by existing billboards. Programmes and use are to be determined by the relationship between image space and physical space.

C = Territories 1, 2, 3, 4. Four existing small public spaces are adapted to form part of the overall structure of Vauxhall X.

D = Crossings 1, 2, 3, 4, 5. Existing viaduct arches create varied relationships between space and objects.

E = Station junction. A linear structure spans the existing platforms from the river junction to the landscape junction.

F = Landscape junction. An adaptation of Spring Gardens provides topographic enclosures and points of reference within the existing landscape.

G = Other. Pavilions, river markers and screens.

Site

The quarter-mile circle is centred on the southern end of Vauxhall Bridge, an area that contains diverse forms of divisions. Physically divided by the Thames and the railway viaduct, it is also socially divided from north to south. In addition, local divisions exist between institutional buildings and public space. There are four key structures or sites adjacent to Vauxhall Bridge: what was the British Gas tower to the northwest; the Government Office for London to the northeast; the Effra site to the southeast; and the MI6 to the southwest. A residential complex is currently under construction on the Effra site, which was a coach park in 1997. The British Gas tower was being converted into residential units at the time of the project and these have now been completed.

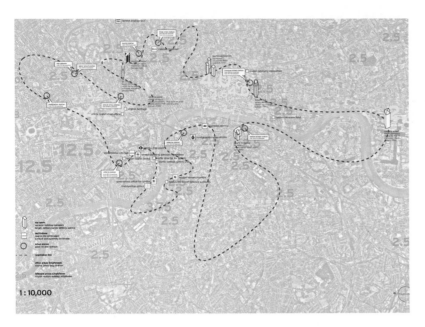

1:10,000

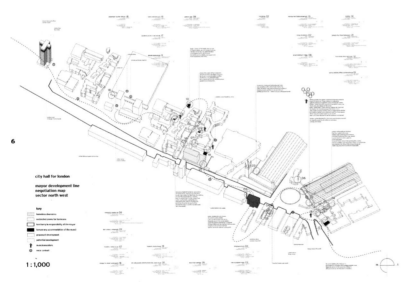

6

city hall for london

mayor development line
negotiation map
sector north west

key

1:1,000

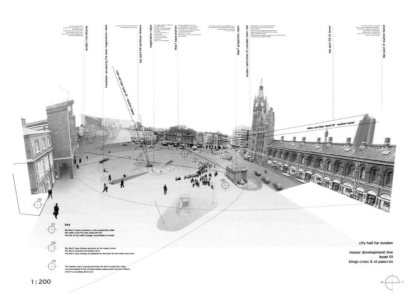

city hall for london

mayor development line
bowl 01
kings cross & st pancras

1:200

CITY HALL
Henrik Rothe and Ole Scheeren

This thesis project and prize-winning competition entry for the 'Design a building for the GLA' competition, London, 1999, proposed a hybrid and decentralised structure to implement the strategies of the new city government. To separate and connect the multiple elements of the city hall, a continuous line of fixed projects and negotiated trajectories is constructed. This line acts as a tool for specific and focused interventions within the city fabric. It establishes a line of negotiation with people and individual conditions and gradually covers the whole territory of the city.

Manifesto

A series of terms describing the phenomena of media space and physical space are introduced to identify social, territorial and economic value systems.

Split mayor: The separation of the representational and operational roles of the mayor is far more efficient than their uncontrolled overlap: liberated from the need to be popular in the conventional sense, the mayor and experts can act in a focused and targeted way and execute the necessary steps to maintain and improve the city structure.

MexT (free negotiable level): Urban negotiators establish lines of relationships and connections between the heterogeneous parts of the city. The lines and trajectories are in constant flux, gradually covering the entire terrain of Greater London.

Vocs (eye level): Representational systems are developed to fully exploit the power of the image: strategic media implementations conceived as hybrids of everyday life and city-government information form a system of virtual communication.

Fixpoints (u level): Excavated from the ground of the city, seven urban arenas create spaces without precise determination, public assembly points and spaces of transience which act as the departure and arrival points of the MexT.

Fixpoints (ad level): Leased by the GLA from commercial institutions, large-scale communication screens at these locations provide information on the city's government and finance.

Fixpoints (sky level): Empty office space in London's seven tallest structures is allocated to the GLA and gives the public access to the sky level of London.

Mayor (super-professional level): Moving between the different locations, the mayor crosses all territories.

mediating and connecting the heterogeneous parts of the City Hall.

Split citizen: The integration of the citizen as private persona and public actor into the governmental process confronts the scale of administrative structure with that of the individual.

Manifest in Vauxhall X and City Hall are the possible relationships between social and physical structures. Both projects acknowledge and use actions, forces, images and multiple interventions to create the proposed spatial configurations.

Actions control social and physical structures

Actions initially form part of an immersion process which identifies the true context for the potential interventions and then sets up the parameters for possible change. For instance, Vauxhall X constructs a conceptual quarter-mile circle of potential, identifies particular institutions, individuals and spatial conditions within it, and records them by means of formal interviews and/or set-up photographs. In contrast, City Hall conceives and identifies a potential social line and verifies it by means of video-recorded interviews with institutions and individuals. Both these participatory actions establish the social and physical territory of intervention. Actions, whether constructed or collaborative, are used from inception to completion as part of the proposed social structures.

Forces influence and shape resultant urban transformations

Whereas Vauxhall X identifies the forces of the major local and informal institutions and includes them in the design process and eventual interventions, City Hall harnesses the current political forces, combines them with precise commercial value systems and reintroduces them into the city. Both projects acknowledge and exploit the existing and potential forces of change and integrate them into the final proposals.

Images form an integral part of the urban reality

Vauxhall X exploits the spatial qualities generated by billboard images and experiments with their inclusion in the design of conceptual, desired and real spaces. City Hall uses the

proposed communication screen as a commercial backdrop of images which allows a secondary use as a means of social and political communication. Whether for political, commercial, communication or conceptual reasons, in both projects, images form part of the architectural language of the proposed spaces.

Multiple interventions are heterogeneous and more closely linked to the urban condition than conventional architectural projects.

Vauxhall X establishes a quarter-mile circle of potential by interacting with spaces, institutions and individuals for a set period of two months. This active involvement, based on arbitrary but personal contacts, crosses existing boundaries, challenges existing divisions and defines a unified structure of public space. This constructed space informs the design process of a series of interventions that make up a three-dimensional and composite urban space governed by both programmed and informal use.

City Hall recognises the relationship between citywide political and legislative changes and their effect at a local scale. It exploits the split representational and operative roles of the mayor in order to generate the alternative institution and space of the city hall. This link between the institution and its space allows City Hall to be flexible enough to interact simultaneously with the individual and the city as a whole.

The exploitation of changing forces, the appropriation of existing spaces, the fragmentation of territory, the manipulation of images and the combination of social and physical interventions create the possibility of a conceptual and reactive urban space. Vauxhall X and City Hall are both combinations of social and physical structures that suggest ways of participating in the social, political, economic and cultural realities of the city, and set out options for designing and inhabiting active urban and spatial strategies within the changing fabric of London. ◬

Carlos Villanueva Brandt is a founding member of NATO (Narrative Architecture Today). He is Diploma 10 Unit Master at the Architectural Association and a visiting lecturer/professor at the Royal College of Art, London. Henrik Rothe and Ole Scheeren were taught by Brandt at the AA, where they collaborated on their diploma project.

Connections Could
Detecting Situationist Tendencies

Julia Chance rises to the challenge that Adriaan Geuze of West 8 poses when he evasively answers her question regarding the influence of situationist thought on his practice. She looks specifically at the situationist notion of 'ambience' in

Be Made There:
in Adriaan Geuze and West 8

West 8's Carrascoplein Shadow Park in Amsterdam and focuses on
the interpretation of boundaries and territories in their design for
the Schouwburgplein in central Rotterdam.

'Connections could be made there.' This was the characteristically enigmatic response from Adriaan Geuze when asked whether he has been influenced by the ideas of the situationists. There are indeed a number of connections to be made, two of which are pursued here by particular interpretations of the Carrascoplein Shadow Park and the Schouwburgplein urban square designed by Adriaan Geuze and West 8. The Carrascoplein, located on the periphery of Amsterdam, detects and develops particular qualities of ambience in an exterior space of the city. The Schouwburgplein, in central Rotterdam, relates to the New Babylonian idea that, through the urban dweller's imaginative interaction with the city, boundaries defining territories may be understood not as being fixed but rather as elements that transform in response to the desires and moods of the city dweller, the random events of the city and environmental changes that occur over time.

Ambience

The Carrascoplein Shadow Park (see previous page) is located beneath the elevated railway tracks leading to the Sloterdijk railway station on the outskirts of Amsterdam. In daylight, well over half the park is in linear stripes of shadow cast by the railway lines overhead. It lies between ill-defined patches of lawn, access roads and car parks, around which an incoherent collection of brash new office buildings are distributed. A number of people walk through the park during the course of the day making their way to and from the offices and the railway station, but at any one time there are rarely more than a couple of people within it.

The project was commissioned by the City of Amsterdam and constructed in 1998. Although only one-third of the proposal by West 8 was carried out, the intention to develop a sense of ambience out of the existing qualities of the site, rather than to impose a new order upon it, is clear. The latter option, for example the creation of an inward-looking garden or a contained playground, would perhaps have been a more predictable response to such a fragmented site.

West 8's proposal for the Carrascoplein deliberately intertwines natural and man-made elements to construct what at first sight appears to be the remnants of a gleefully artificial wooded landscape. The ground surface of the park is arranged according to a graphic pattern of grass and asphalt areas strewn with identical cast-iron models of tree stumps which are lit up from within at night to glow and cast shadows over the columns and undersides of the overhead bridges. One of the smooth concrete columns supporting the railway overhead has metamorphosed into a textured tree trunk and at intermittent intervals trains roar past overhead. There are no fences or other devices to mark the boundaries of the park, and its parameters are understood by the distance to which the rusting iron tree stumps can be seen to extend.

By acknowledging rather than rejecting the particular qualities of ambience in the Carrascoplein, the sensibility of West 8 bears similarities to that of the situationists, who on their urban drifts noted areas with such qualities of ambience: similarly unpeopled external spaces, located far from the sites of the spectacle, through which one could literally drift. The Carrascoplein is certainly not a project whose formal qualities can be considered at a distance, but it is a scenario in which you are physically immersed.

The view of manufactured tree stumps strewn across a grass and asphalt carpet may at first glance be interpreted as being gleefully artificial, a playful representation of nature in the city as yet another scenario constructed for straightforward pleasure. On a prolonged visit however, and particularly in darkness when the site is often empty, there is a sense of unease in the atmosphere, a more complex aesthetic created by the severed and glowing tree stumps that surround one, casting shadows over the concrete columns and flyovers as trains roar overhead.

In *The Architectural Uncanny* , Anthony Vidler proposes that the sense of the uncanny (as theoretically pursued by Freud) can be placed 'centrally among the categories that might be adduced to interpret modernity and especially its conditions of spatiality, architectural and urban'. The state of estrangement, unhomeliness, is a contemporary cultural predicament and one that has developed from its original medium of literature into a number of architectural projects that are assessed by Vidler. The psychogeographical qualities of the Carrascoplein can also be considered with reference to Freud's theory of the uncanny. 'The uncanny is that class of the frightening which leads back to what is known of old and long familiar.'

Freud investigated the ambiguity inherent in the meaning of the German word *unheimlich* (unhomely, uncanny) and its apparent opposite, *heimlich* (originally homely, now meaning to be secret, concealed). The interchangeability of the words and his further investigations led him to the conclusion that, 'an uncanny experience occurs either when infantile complexes which have been repressed are once more revived by some impression, or when primitive beliefs which have been surmounted seem once more to be confirmed.'

Amongst his examples of potential triggers to uncanny feelings, Freud refers to how the effects of darkness, silence and solitude are fears that everyone experiences in childhood, as well as to how the image or description of dismembered limbs may arouse repressed fears of castration which will, to different degrees, be repressed or surmounted in adulthood. He also refers to the potentially uncanny effect of an object that leaves a sense of ambiguity as to whether it is inanimate or animate – for example, a doll or waxwork that seems as though it might actually come to life: 'Dismembered limbs, a severed head, a hand cut off at the wrist, as in feet which dance by themselves ... all of these have something particularly uncanny about them, especially when [...] they prove capable of independent activity in addition.'

Reference to Freud's theory of the uncanny (which is more complex than can be discussed here) indicates posssible reasons why the sight of a number of apparently inanimate, man-made tree stumps, which are severed near their bases and strewn across a generally unpeopled area and which also 'come to life' in the darkness with glowing lights appearing from within, may create a particular ambience that triggers a sense of unease.

The Carrascoplein is a critical project which, by working with a situationist sensibility for valuing qualities of ambience perceived in the existing cityscape, makes the sense of estrangement, the unhomeliness of the surroundings, more visible and as such criticises the conditions from which it emerged.

Boundaries and Territories

Boundaries within New Babylon were to be flexible and responsive to the changing desires of its inhabitants, and in the 'Naked City' map – Guy Debord's famous graphic representation of the giant situationist playground of the city of Paris –the importance of boundaries and contained territories was communicated by the care with which each of the urban fragments was cut out. However, on the map the area between the cut-outs remained flexible; the large red arrows in the map could bend and stretch as required between the floating fragments. There was plenty of room for the possible extension or reduction of each urban cut-out in response to the subject's changing perception of the city, and the map was a representation of the city as perceived at a particular moment in time. Urban boundaries in the 'Naked City' map and in the everyday life of the New Babylonian were thus subject to change and were located between the physical realm of the city fabric and the imagination of the subject.

There is something paradoxical about trying to construct the conditions for play through design; everyone knows that as a child the best place for playing was not the school playground but a location that was not specifically designed for this; territories which it became possible to appropriate through imaginative activity, regardless of where they were and to whom

they belonged. In psychological terms, the existence of boundaries is important to contain any playful activity, but such boundaries are only fixed until there is a new idea, a change in mood or until the game is played out. They bear little or no relation to anything as banal as a property law.

On West 8's Schouwburgplein, the expanse of the square is divided into different areas by the means of different surface textures: perforated galvanised steel panels, timber boarding, epoxy, box-section steel grille and a strip of rubber are composed to make up the 12,250-square-metre area. The junctions between different surface materials are utilised as boundaries to contain both spontaneous and organised activities within them; games of five-a-side football on the timber-boarded surface and rollerblading over the

Above
View looking south over
the Schouwburgplein.

Notes
1. Extract from an exchange
between Julia Chance and
Adriaan Geuze, Rotterdam
(21 July 2000).
2. Anthony Vidler, *The
Architectural Uncanny*, MIT
Press (Cambridge, Mass),
1992, p 12.
3. Sigmund Freud, *Art and
Literature*, Pelican (London),
1985, p 340.
4. Ibid, p 372.
5. Ibid, p 366.

epoxy. The rubber strip is used to mark out a thoroughfare from one side of the square to another.

The junctions between the different surface textures of the square are designed to be flush with one another, so that while the territories and boundaries between materials and areas of play are clearly inscribed they are also easily transgressed, dissolving in response to changing activities in the surrounding areas or to a change of mood or idea by games players themselves. People occupying the Schouwburgplein arrange themselves around one another in a continual state of negotiation and oscillation, with reference to, but without being controlled by, the boundaries suggested by the composition of the surface materials.

As well as providing the opportunity for such reciprocal interaction between city fabric, individual desire and group behaviour, the surface of the square transforms over time, between daylight and darkness, both in terms of the boundaries inscribed and the qualities of the surfaces themselves. Strip lighting is installed beneath the steel panels and seeps through their perforations, transforming them into a shimmering plateau; the strip of box-section steel, which is barely noticeable in daylight, appears as a prominent bright green river which throws any passing body into a sculpted vision of moving light and shadow. The intense light distributed by the overhead spotlights after dark creates new clearly defined territories on the surface of the square. These overlay the previous territories marked out in timber, rubber and steel panels, and the new territories attract new occupants.

Boundaries defined in daylight are thus rearranged in darkness, instigating new kinds of occupation. Also, by an elegant device, in case any of the territories inscribed on the square's surface are in danger of becoming too heavily etched in the minds of the users – perhaps dominated by one group for too long – they are intermittently disrupted by blasts of movement from the spotlights. In response either to a coin inserted by a member of the public or to a preprogrammed random dance, the lights sporadically, energetically and messily scribble over the orthogonal geometric composition of the other surface materials.

Thus the Schouwburgplein creates a flexible and responsive city fabric in keeping with Constant's New Babylon project. It is not only that the surface of the square is designed to accommodate temporary structures, or simply that the bases of the enormous spotlights can move. Rather more interestingly, it is also the way in which a reciprocal relationship can exist between the imaginative faculties of those who are enjoying playful activities, who require boundaries which can be subject to change, and the surfaces of the city on which they play – and it is the potential the square has for responsive interaction between the individual, the group, the random event within city life and the transformations over time between daylight and darkness. ♺

Julia Chance is an architect.

What is the difference between a Situationist and an Essex girl?

In playful mood, General Lighting & Power rally against the hegemonic posturings of *laissez-faire* capitalism and construct a world where joy and pleasure are the main constituents of everyday life.

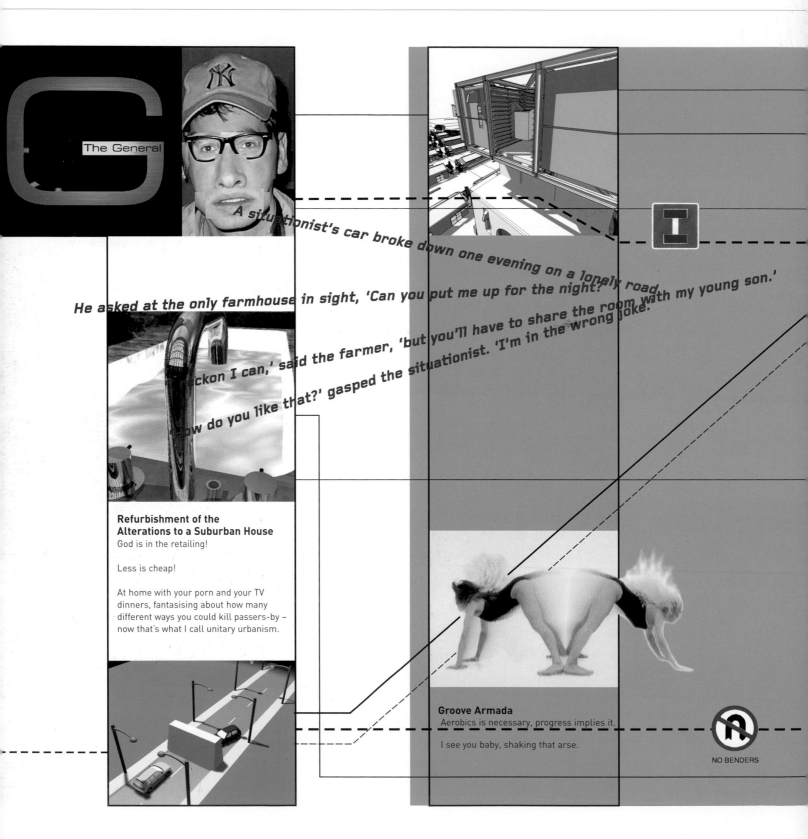

The General

A situationist's car broke down one evening on a lonely road. He asked at the only farmhouse in sight, 'Can you put me up for the night?' 'I reckon I can,' said the farmer, 'but you'll have to share the room with my young son.' 'How do you like that?' gasped the situationist. 'I'm in the wrong joke.'

Refurbishment of the Alterations to a Suburban House

God is in the retailing!

Less is cheap!

At home with your porn and your TV dinners, fantasising about how many different ways you could kill passers-by – now that's what I call unitary urbanism.

Groove Armada

Aerobics is necessary, progress implies it.

I see you baby, shaking that arse.

NO BENDERS

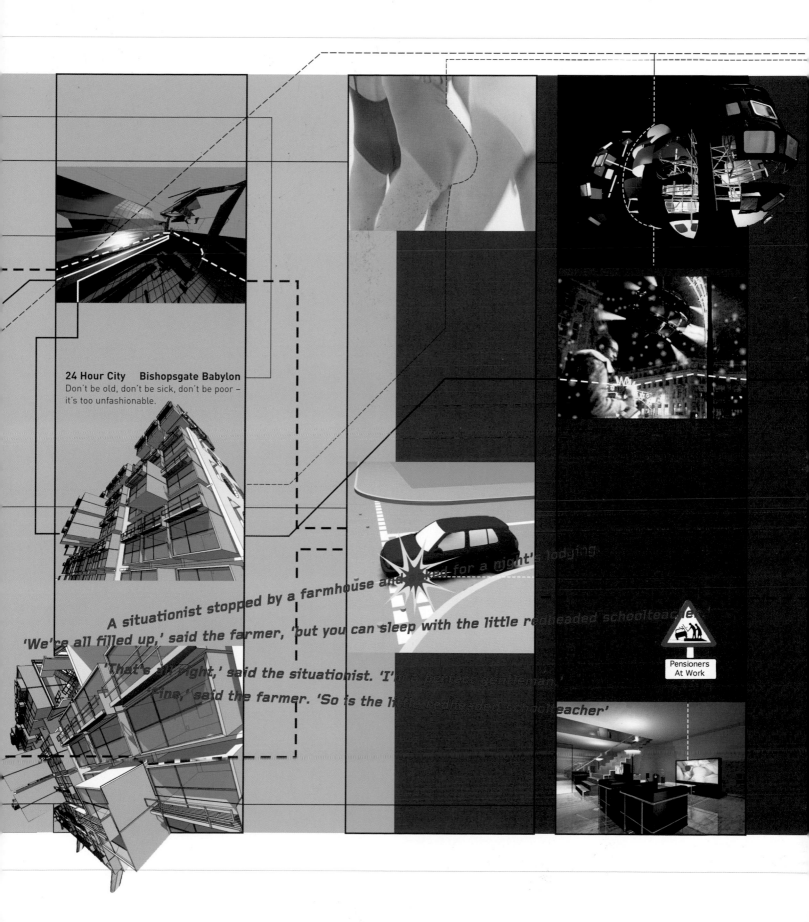

24 Hour City   Bishopsgate Babylon
Don't be old, don't be sick, don't be poor –
it's too unfashionable.

Pensioners
At Work

A situationist stopped by a farmhouse and asked for a night's lodging.
'We're all filled up,' said the farmer, 'but you can sleep with the little redheaded schoolteacher.'
'That's all right,' said the situationist. 'I'm a perfect gentleman.'
'Fine,' said the farmer. 'So is the little redheaded schoolteacher'

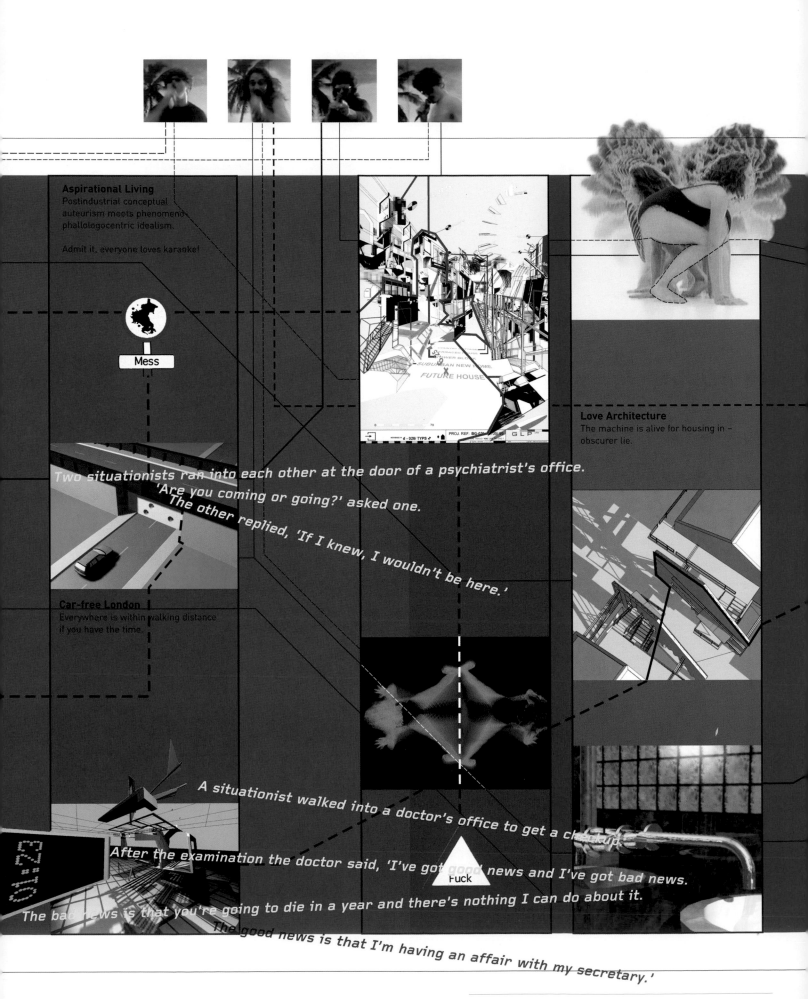

Aspirational Living
Postindustrial conceptual auteurism meets phenomeno-phallologocentric idealism.

Admit it, everyone loves karaoke!

Mess

Love Architecture
The machine is alive for housing in – obscurer lie.

Two situationists ran into each other at the door of a psychiatrist's office. 'Are you coming or going?' asked one. The other replied, 'If I knew, I wouldn't be here.'

Car-free London
Everywhere is within walking distance if you have the time.

A situationist walked into a doctor's office to get a checkup. After the examination the doctor said, 'I've got good news and I've got bad news. The bad news is that you're going to die in a year and there's nothing I can do about it. The good news is that I'm having an affair with my secretary.'

Fuck

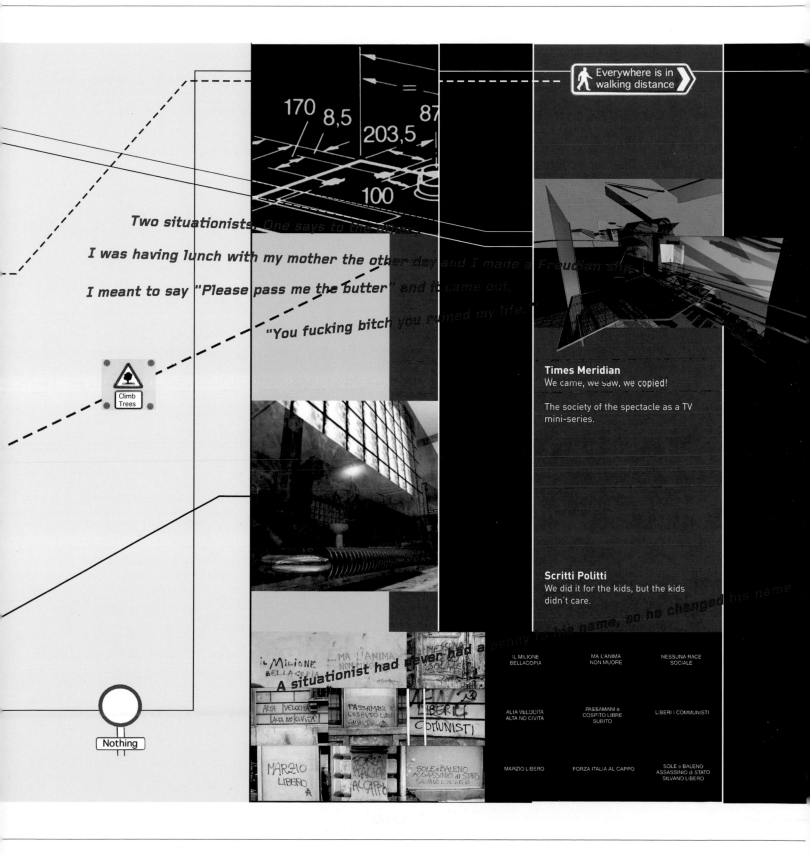

Everywhere is in walking distance

170 8,5   87
203,5
100

Two situationists. One says to the other,

I was having lunch with my mother the other day and I made a Freudian slip.

I meant to say "Please pass me the butter" and it came out,

"You fucking bitch you ruined my life."

Climb Trees

Times Meridian
We came, we saw, we copied!

The society of the spectacle as a TV mini-series.

Scritti Politti
We did it for the kids, but the kids didn't care.

A situationist had never had a penny to his name, so he changed his name.

Nothing

IL MILIONE BELLACOPIA	MA L'ANIMA NON MUORE	NESSUNA RACE SOCIALE
ALIA VELUCITA ALTA NO CIVITA	PASSAMANI e COSPITO LIBRE SUBITO	LIBERI I COMUNISTI
MARZIO LIBERO	FORZA ITALIA AL CAPPO	SOLE e BALENO ASSASSINIO di STATO SILVANO LIBERO

Manoeuvre:
Discursive Performance

Parallels can be drawn between the manoeuvres or guided walking tours executed by the artist Tim Brennan and the *dérives* or drifts of the situationist project. Similarly, Brennan seeks to raise consciousness and 'speak' to his participants through his tours, which combine highlights of 'ideologically unselfconscious phenomena' with 'bodies of pre-existing information'.

Opposite page
'The photograph shows how unexpected significance can occur in the public process of Tim Brennan's work. Taken outside Leeds Town Hall on Tim's tour "Shepherds of Arcadia, Leeds 2000", the image shows cardboard boxes laid flat on the ground behind the town hall columns. At the top of the picture are the legs of the people on the tour (or "manoeuvre"). At this point in the tour Tim was relating (from the *Yorkshire Post* of 1936) how the Jarrow Marchers were accommodated at Leeds Town Hall and acknowledging the providers of bedding. The flattened boxes we found were another person's bedding.'
Gary Kirkham, photographer, December 2000.

Above left
Chinatown, Manchester.

Above right
Grosvenor Square, Manchester.

Stalker: 'The Zone's a very complex maze of traps. All of them are death traps. I don't know what happens here in the absence of humans but as soon as humans appear, everything begins to move. Former traps disappear, new ones appear. Safe ways become impassable and the way becomes now easy, now confused beyond words.'

I have been working with the form of organised walking for five years. I refer to these walks as manoeuvres. They exist in a region between traditions of performance art, the historical tour, loco-descriptive poetry, pilgrimage, expanded notions of sculpture and plain old pedestrianism. Each walk is constructed solely from quotations which do not always illustrate, or satisfy, the expected histories of a route. The use of pre-existing material is important in that the collision of quoted texts with seemingly unrelated sites wrenches the viewer into thought, enabling them into a reflexive mode of expanded reading. Nothing is 'easy' or 'comfortable' in this situation; the work exists as either an awkward, seemingly didactic art activity or an act of anti-academic plagiarism. The formal nature of each walk makes no claim to an essentialist or naturalised authorship. Each quote is consciously read aloud and at times participants (other walkers, bystanders) are invited to recite sections. This accumulative process constitutes

a material transparency, the construction of which exists as an act of curation (it involves my value judgements as selector of words and directions within a taxonomical frame).

The manoeuvre can be understood as expanded sculpture. Although it sits in antithesis to the fixed object, it subsumes into its horizon line the three-dimensional presence of material such as sculpture, painting, architecture, the monument, and everyday phenomena such as cars, kerbs, trees, tin cans, people, the weather, etc. The diverse logic of aesthetic discourses is therefore incorporated in each manoeuvre in an unselfconscious fashion.

Stalker: 'This is the Zone. It might seem capricious but at each moment it's just as we've made it by our state of mind.'

Recent academic research has tended to shift analyses of place away from the politics of essence, locatedness and specificity to notions of hybridity, intertextuality and dislocation, and to an understanding of the past as a web of conflicting and often disjointed factional narrations. The sociality of space, which makes it a 'place', is just the 'trace' of 'human' intentionality. Through walking one can come to understand place as a built environment of texts, and within this context each walk I produce exists as a manoeuvring through the politics of space and time as language.

The manoeuvre was therefore constructed within this disjunction. I wanted to find a way of opening the artwork up to the pitfalls and footfalls, fragments and half glimpses that form our perception of the past and

Above and opposite
Junction of Hulme Street and
Oxford Road, Manchester.

Notes
1. Andrei Tarkovsky, *Stalker*,
Mosfilm Studio, 1979.
2. manoeuvre v.t. & i. Also
manoeuver. L18 [Fr.
manoeuvrer f. med. L
man(u)operare from L. manu
operari work with the hand. f.
manus hand.] (cause to)
perform a manoeuvre or
manoeuvres; move or steer by
an act of control requiring
some skill; employ or effect a
stratagem or artifice; act or
manipulate schemingly or
adroitly. (Foll. By into, out of,
etc.). *Collins English
Dictionary*.
3. In this sense the manoeuvre
might be understood as a
movement through the entire
expanded field as developed by
Rosalind Krauss in her famous
essay 'Sculpture in the

the reflection of our multiple selves. I chose to
work with the form of the guided walk, primarily
because it evaded the fixity of the site-specific
object and the body-centred performance. This
involves travelling.

The manoeuvre is open to phenomena.
As a mode it has no beginning and end. It
includes variances in the climate, weather
and temperature, and fluctuations in the levels
of noise and light. It allows for the divergence
of a participant's memory or that of the accrued
experience which they automatically bring to
the event structure. Manoeuvres are not
interventions but are rather open to the
intervention of everyday life; a car collided with
a cyclist in the course of my most recent work.
Each walk of intention operates as a historical
implement within an expanded process of
writing and reading.

By exploring narrations through a locale,
a participant wroughts the substance of a
particular terrain, adding to the accretion of
experience that forms any environment. The
individual/group inscribes its way through a
polyphony of discourses, the nexus of which
is provided by the web of selected texts.

**Stalker: 'I won't hide the fact that some
people had to turn back halfway. There were
some who perished on the very threshold of the
Room. But everything that happens here
depends not on the Zone, but on us.'**

'Reading Capital' is an ongoing project involving
existing English editions of Karl Marx's *Das Kapital* as
ad hoc guidebooks. By introducing a map into the sleeve
of each *Das Kapital* it is possible to marry grid
references with textual passages to prompt the reader
into an investigation of the geopolitical terrain. The
work lies in the interstice between a book which might
interpret the entire world and the *idea* of a book which
might interpret the entire world. It investigates histories
of currency through pecuniary to abstract credit, from
instrumental tool to commodity artwork and the
information highway. So, for example, in 'Reading
Capital #1: A Decimal Dance', produced for the
exhibition 'You Are Here', the combination of map,
coordinates, citations and book form a guidebook with
which the participant may explore Manchester city
centre through the optic of Das Kapital. My role as a live
guide is subtracted in this work so as to enable the
quicker emergence of a depersonalised generic model
that can be applied to any spatial situation in the known
(mapped) world. This might then be elaborated via the
Web and through the use of a global positioning system
to activate readings of the text.

It is possible to imagine a process of reading and
rereading that mirrors the duration of writing. It is
proposed that 'Reading Capital' will correspond to the
approximate length of time it took Marx to arrive at his
text – nine years. Over time a library of *Das Kapitals* will
be accumulated, each with a particular modification
particular to a locale that might initiate a participant's
orientation from near or far. The collection of one book

Expanded Field', *October* 8
(Spring 1979), pp 30–44. My
practice exists within a
different historical moment to
that explored by Krauss and in
this context the apparatus of
the manoeuvre is only
beginning to be critically
understood.
4. Tarkovsky, op cit.
5. See Doreen Massey 'Places
and Their Pasts', *History
Workshop Journal*, 39, 1995,
p 183.
6. Tarkovsky, op cit.
7. Karl Marx, *Das Kapital*, first
published 1867.
8. Tarkovsky, op cit.
9. 'You Are Here', Holden
Gallery, Manchester
Metropolitan University, 2000;
curated by Graham Parker.
10. Mikhail Bakhtin, *Formy
vremi I khronatopa v romane*,
1937–8. English translation:
'Forms of the Chronotope in
the Novel' in Michael Holquist
(ed), *Dialogic Imagination*,
University of Texas Press
(Austin), 1981, pp 84–258.
11. For a fuller investigation
into heteroglossia see Bakhtin,
The Dialogical Principle, trans
Wlad Godizich: Theory and
History of Literature, vol 13,
Manchester University Press
(Manchester), 1984, p 56.
12. Tarkovsky, op cit.
For a further consideration of
organised walking in relation
to 'stalking' see Chris Jenks 'A
Walk on the East Side' in Tim
Brennan (ed) *Guidebook:
Three Manouvres by Tim
Brennan in London E1/E2*,
Camerawork (London), 1998.

instils a further enquiry into the processes and
conventions of ring-fencing knowledge for
inspection.

The manoeuvre attempts to resist approaches
that sever art from life, theory from practice,
writing from reading, interpretation from
production, mimesis from actuality and past
from present from future. In its attempt to draw
on a wide range of voices and construct
temporary gaps for critical distance, the work is
unbound from the conventions of the art world.

**Professor (Scientist): 'So the Zone lets the
good through and kills the evil?'[9]**

The manoeuvre utilises found materials and
texts to assemble the possibility for a particular
chronotope, by which I mean a modelling
organisation of time and space which engages
with historical contexts.[10] In this way sites can
be defined as chronotopes (chronos meaning
time, topos meaning place or topic [in
discourse]). A walk of intention manoeuvres
through space and time forming a web of
interrelated chronotopes (websites) amounting
to what might be termed heteroglossia.[11]

My role in each of these walks is that of
grammarian as opposed to conventional 'guide'
and involves me in a process of highlighting
ideologically unselfconscious phenomena and
'pointing out' bodies of pre-existing information.
Out of textual material the possibilities of a
parallel intertextual work of imagination are

opened to the participants. These works/walks are
intellectually organic, each involving active participation
from a wide range of individuals whilst retaining a
pedagogic aspect.

Within a discursive performance of this kind the
production of meaning does not depend on the
subjectivity of any one walker. Through the use of real
space and time the engagement of the group in
constructing chronotopes involves an absence of
authorship, and a process of construction of subjectivity
which could be laid bare and examined in terms of its
blockages, ironies, dissonances, collective
dependencies and radical and inescapable historicality.

**Stalker: 'I'm not sure. I think it lets those through
who've lost all hope; not good or bad but the wretched.
But even the most wretched will perish if they don't
know how to behave here.'[12]** ᴀᴅ

Artist Tim Brennan is Curator of Talks and Critical Events at Project,
Dublin, and his forthcoming monograph will be entitled *Chronograph*,
(ed) John Gange, 2001

51

Abstract

Tours Operator

Laura Ruggeri describes her Abstract Tours project of 1997 in which she organised a series of detournements – destabilising spectacles – from a Portakabin in East Berlin. Parodying conventional sightseeing tours, they ignored all given routes and took their form from random geometric figures laid over a printed map.

In 1997 I operated a 'tour agency' from a Portakabin placed in Schlossplatz, formerly known as Marx-Engelsplatz, a central square in Berlin. For a month I sat there offering 'geometrical tours' of the city to both visitors and locals.

Tour routes were 'designed' by the participants themselves, with the help of Perspex stencils placed at random on a map of Berlin[2] – a regulated use of chance that ensured that none of the patterns would generate the same route. People were encouraged to follow their itinerary as closely as possible and to the best of their physical abilities; in order to 'stick to the line' some would jump over fences, cut through private properties, climb over walls, cross railway lines. Others chose to swerve from their route in order to dodge obstacles.

All participants were invited to document their experience and play an active role in organising the exhibition that took place in the Künstlerhaus Bethanien[3] a month later. Around 45 people, among whom were Stalker,[4] accepted my invitation and contributed videos, photographs, sketches, found objects, logbooks, audio recordings and journals. Others simply turned up to share their experiences in the forum discussion that took place alongside the exhibition. During this event I discovered that one group performing the tour with a crowbar, ropes and other climbers' gear had been intercepted by the police and questioned for hours; two people had wandered on to a private golf course (which did not feature on any map!) and stolen the balls that were later exhibited as trophies; members of Stalker had marked their route by leaving a trail of flour behind them (an action that also prompted someone to call the police); a Czech tourist had persuaded an old German lady to let him into her house on the grounds that it was on his route; and a Berlin resident spent hours inside Schering, the pharmaceutical company, successfully dodging their security guards.

Cracking the code (on the ground)

Abstract Tours parodied the idea of a Stadtrundgang (German for 'sightseeing tour', literally meaning a 'round-city tour') by literalising it and suggesting possible geometrical variants such as triangular, square or trapezoidal tours. The gesture of drawing a geometrical pattern on the map also parodied the modernist's conceit that 'the transcendental forces of geometry must prevail' (Le Corbusier). It mimicked the

conceptual abstractions that inform the
configuration of spatial practices such as
architecture and city planning, the design of
routes, the schematic grid of property lines and,
last but not least, the construction
of the infamous Berlin Wall.

By walking along lines traced on paper rather
than realised on the ground with a wrecking ball
and reinforced concrete, abstract tourism aimed
to expose a code rather than imitate it, an
inverse rather than a symmetrical practice.
One could trace the geometric shapes that
constituted the kernel of the architectural
redesign by the act of walking them.

The choice of abstraction had been made
in order to expose, rather than conceal, an
imposition – a framing process that imposes its
vision – generated elsewhere in the political
and economic field where groups that have
'inherited' the city have a claim on its symbolic
spaces. At the time that I was working on
Abstract Tours Berlin's identity was being
redefined by the re-establishment of its capital
status and the restoration of its pre-Wall plan in
a central and crucial area of the city. This urban
fabric was being transformed by the juxtaposed

interests of multinational companies as investors, and
by the space requirements for the new parliament and
federal government buildings.

A heuristic device
Abstract geometric tours cut through the city, intersect
with discrete terrains, establish unfamiliar links and
reverse the dominant trend towards fragmentation,
separation and disintegration of urban space. Based on
chance, the points, lines and areas establish a different
syntax of sites. This opens up the state of enclosure
that has been preconditioned by a tourist industry that
proliferates historical revisions, idealises urban space
and creates selective landscapes for consumption.

By following his or her line line a participant
encounters the residual, interstitial, 'banal' spaces
that are ignored by tourist narratives: penetrable and
impenetrable buildings, residential areas, warehouses
and sweatshops, industrial estates, construction sites
where workers speak foreign languages, cemeteries,
playgrounds... Geometric tourism exposes the
construction of the tourist attraction as inextricably
bound up in the notion of contrast and difference.

Tourism is widely conceived as an opposite
to work, and the practice of travel takes tourists away
from the familiarity of places of employment or

Abstract Tours operator,
Schlossplatz, Berlin, 1997.
The porta cabin stood between
Palast der Republik (once
home of the East German
legislature, now abandoned)
and the Staatsratsgebäude
(where projects for the
corporate reshaping of the
capital are exhibited to the
public).

residence and into ones that have been selected as providing varying levels of contrast to the familiar. Like any form of production, tourism has reshaped the city. Traditional strategies of coherence have been eroded through compression and condensation; our experience of a city has been flattened out to an easily digestible narrative.

Abstract Tourism did not single out isolated historical buildings of 'touristic value', but stressed instead the relationship between buildings. It did not highlight Die Mauer (the remains of the Berlin Wall left standing for tourists), but played an operative role in revealing the countless walls, fences and obstacles hindering public access throughout the city. A geometric route both 'suppresses' and submits to the dimensions of reality. It generates a set of conditions that disclose the confinement rather than creating illusions of freedom.

Abstract dérives?
The situationists recommended that urban space be navigated *à la dérive*, that is drifting through varied ambiences. The technique revolved around the idea that, through the instinctual exploration of the emotional contours of one's environment, playful and anti-authoritarian places and journeys can be discovered or created. The practice of the dérive involved an unstructured wandering through the landscape, allowing oneself to be drawn consciously and unconsciously towards those sites and movements that heighten one's experience of place and disrupt the banality of one's everyday life.

Some critics have described Abstract Tourism as a type of dérive, pointing out the similarities between my project and this practice. I personally think Abstract Tours is more closely related to another situationist practice, that of détournement, as theorised by Raoul Vaneigem, which involves taking elements from a given system and turning them against it, a parodic destabilisation of the spectacle that exposes its alienating effects. Although I can subscribe to the situationist programme insofar as it rejects a specialised notion of cultural production and the institutionalisation of the creative process, I have a few reservations about the viability of the dérives in our present situation.

In fact I think of Abstract Tours as a critique of the dérives. This is not intended to be a dismissal of the practice; rather, the tours were a critical development of a practice that was, after all, theorised in 1956! They

Notes
1. The Portakabin stood between Palast der Republik (once home of the East German legislature, now abandoned) and the Staatsratsgebäude (where projects for the corporate reshaping of the capital are exhibited to the public).
2. The maps (scale 1: 5,000) were obtained from the Land Registry and covered all

ABSTRAKTE REISEN

districts of Berlin.

3. Located in a 19th-century complex of former hospital buildings, Künstlerhaus Bethanien was originally squatted in the 1970s and at that time hosted alternative art and theatre. Today it offers studio residencies to foreign artists and recipients of Deutscher Akademischer Austausdienst (German Academic Exchange Service) grants.
4. Stalker, a collective subject that engages research and actions within the landscape, had previously been recording and analysing the mutation of the territory around Rome.
5. 'Tacheles, an abandoned department store taken over by squatters. The façade is decorated with scrap-iron and graffiti, like a West Berlin squat of the 1970s. Inside there is a cinema, café and theater; all very rudimentary.' From The American Express Guide to Berlin.
6. Gilles Ivain, 'Formulary for a New Urbanism', Internationale situationniste, no 1 (1958). Republished in Ken Knabb (ed), Situationist International Anthology, Bureau of Public Secrets (Berkeley, Cal), 1981, pp 1–4.

took place some 40 years later, in a city where 'playful and anti-authoritarian places' such as Tacheles feature in mainstream guidebooks,[5] where the 'carnivalesque' is actively promoted by local authorities and where events such as the Love Parade are sponsored by multinationals and contribute to boost the image of Berlin worldwide.

In my opinion the dérives suggested by Debord have lost much of their critical potential as they have become more the norm: consumption has replaced production in most urban areas, both tourists and consumers are actually invited to wander around together in a 'leisurely manner', and the psychological effects of artfully created ambiences are well known to, and exploited by, those who design shopping malls (mercenary psychogeographers?).

The situationists proposed that new maps expressing psychogeographical possibilities and explorations should be drawn up, and this is precisely what guidebooks do by suggesting walks through neighbourhoods and districts that present a 'unity of atmosphere', and organising movements around 'psychogeographic hubs': the 'Bizarre and Sinister Quarters' envisaged by Ivan

Chtcheglov (aka Gilles Ivain) in his 'Formulary for a New Urbanism'[6] have become a reality, as has the 'experimental city' that 'would live largely off tolerated and controlled tourism'.

Tourists, though usually regarded as mere consumers of the city, in fact produce accounts of their experiences, mostly by means of visual texts. These are generally shared only with friends and relatives, but this nonetheless contributes actively to shaping the image of a city within their social and familial circle. ⌀

Laura Ruggeri is a cultural activist and researcher.

Weather
Architecture

Taking his cue from the situationist idea that architecture can
consist of ephemeral conditions and appropriations, Jonathan Hill
uses weather as an intellectual material in a project based
on the reconstructed Barcelona Pavilion of 1986. In so doing,
he challenges architect's elevation of buildings to art objects of
sterile contemplation.

The Barcelona Pavilions

Designed by Mies van der Rohe, the first Barcelona Pavilion was built for an exhibition. Construction began in March 1929 and the building was dismantled in February 1930, its various elements dispersed or destroyed. In 1986 Ignasi de Solà Morales, Christian Cirici and Fernando Ramos supervised the construction of a second pavilion on the site of the first one. The materials of the 1929 pavilion did not always follow Mies' design. For example, on the exterior side and rear walls plastered brick painted green and yellow was used instead of green alpine marble and travertine. Solà Morales, Cirici and Ramos' intention was to recreate the 1929 pavilion as faithfully as possible, but with improvements to those parts of the design that had been compromised by either economic or technical restrictions.

The photographs that established the reputation of the 1929 pavilion only record the parts that followed Mies' design. Photographs of the other parts do not remain and may not have been taken. The subject of the reconstruction is the design as it appears in the original photographs, as much as it is the building constructed in 1929. Architectural photographs have a number of roles, one of which is to present the building as a higher form of cultural production in order to defend and promote architects and patrons. Many of them have similar characteristics, such as perfect climate and no people, in part because they mimic the perfect but sterile viewing conditions of the art gallery. Juan Pablo Bonta writes: 'The effect of the Barcelona Pavilion over the physical or social environment in the hills of Montjuich was negligible; its effect as an idea spread over the entire world by means of photographs and descriptions was enormous.' Between the demolition of the first pavilion in 1930 and the construction of the second in 1986, the Barcelona Pavilion became one of the most praised and copied architectural projects of the 20th century. The 1929 photographs, as much as the 1929 building, were copied. To realise the extent of the appropriation we just need to visualise the pavilion with petrol pumps on its forecourt, a cash machine in the wall or a barbecue by the pool. The extent of this copying is due not only to the quality of the design, and Mies' growing reputation, but also to the pavilion's status as an artwork.

The Contemplation of Architecture

In an attempt to maintain and reproduce the aura of art and the artist, the art institution requires precise codes of behaviour, particularly reverence. Although other experiences are possible, the artwork in a gallery is primarily experienced in contemplation: a form of visual awareness, of a single object by a single absorbed viewer, in which sound, smell and touch are as far as possible eradicated. Protected against heat, light and decay, the artwork is experienced a few times at most. This is not the familiar experience of a building but, for architects, the classification of architecture as an art similar to painting and sculpture is a social and financial necessity. To affirm the status of the architect as an artist and architecture as an art, the experience of the building is equated with the contemplation of an artwork in a gallery, a condition disturbed by the irreverent presence of the user.

Solà Morales, Cirici and Ramos state that the purpose of the reconstruction is to allow the building to be experienced once again, but the experience they describe is contemplation, in which the visitor is absorbed by the artwork:

> It is necessary to go there, to walk amidst and see the startling contrast between the building and its surroundings, to let your gaze be drawn into the calligraphy of the patterned marble and its kaleidoscopic figures, to feel yourself enmeshed in a system of planes in stone, glass and water that envelops and moves you through space, and contemplate the hard, emphatic play of Kolbe's bronze dancer over water.

The Barcelona Pavilion is an architectural icon, not only because it is seductive and much copied, but also because it has most often been perceived in conditions similar to that of the artwork. Between 1929 and 1930 it was an exhibition building to be viewed; between 1930 and 1986, it was known through photographs and since 1986 the reconstruction's status as exhibit, gallery and historical monument discourages everyday use. The history of the pavilion implies that contemplation is the experience most appropriate to buildings, affirming the authority of the architect and denying that of the user.

Water Lilies

As Solà Morales, Cirici and Ramos say they wish to be faithful to the 1929 pavilion, it is interesting to see what they ignored: 'As for the presence of floral elements, it is apparent that the large pool was planted with water lilies, which in due course covered its entire surface, even causing maintenance problems.' The water lilies are absent from the 1986 pavilion. As the architects attempted to resolve other technical problems, I assume that the water lilies were not replanted because they would introduce life to the 1986 pavilion, and an awareness of time, occupation and climate; all incompatible with the experience of a contemplative artwork.

Opposite
Berlin 2.55 pm 18 December 1929; Barcelona 2.55 pm 18 December 1999.
Large pool: calm (Ba), clear sky (Ba); small pool: snow (Be), clear sky (Ba); external travertine floor: fog (Be), clear sky (Ba).

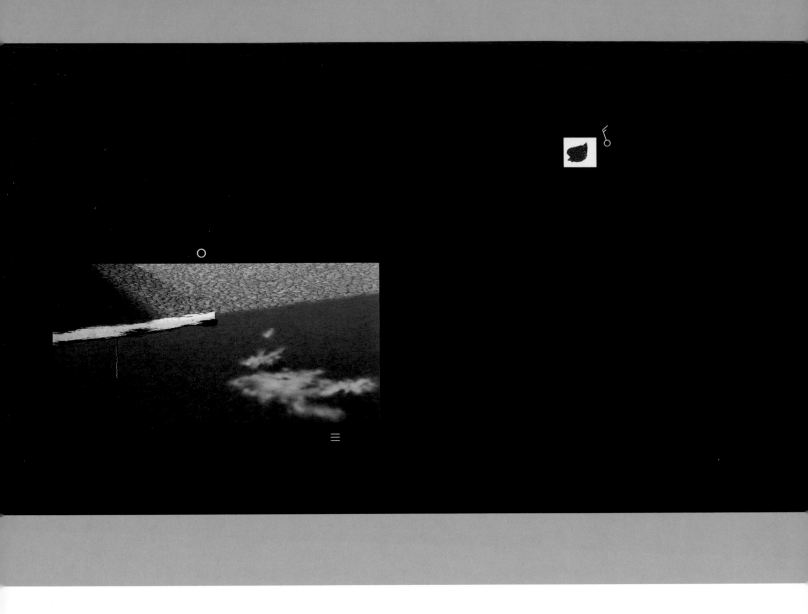

Although it is now commonly known as the Barcelona Pavilion, the building was commissioned by the Weimar Republic and constructed as the German Pavilion for the Barcelona Universal Exposition. But despite its name and its relationship to Germany, the pavilion is more often associated with international modernism. Solà Morales, Cirici and Ramos argue, however, that it has a precise relationship to its site. Maybe one of the purposes of the reconstruction is to emphasise the pavilion's relationship to Barcelona and disregard its connections to Germany and Spain. Two masts, 15.5 metres high, were placed symmetrically in front of the 1929 building. The German flag flew from one of them, the Spanish flag from the other. The size of the flags, each measuring 6 x 9 metres, gave them special prominence. The masts were rebuilt in 1986 but the flags are absent.

An Original Copy

Architects are caught in a vicious circle; in order to emphasise their idea of architecture they often adopt techniques, forms and materials already identified with the work of architects, and learn little from other disciplines. In contrast, I take from art the principle that a space can be made of anything, and from situationism the idea that architecture can consist of ephemeral conditions and appropriations. The exclusion of weather is a fundamental purpose of buildings. But I use weather as an architectural material to introduce what is absent from the 1986 pavilion: habitual occupation, Germany and the passage of time. Mies designed the original pavilion in Berlin. My transformation mimics the weather there between March 1929 and February 1930, and inserts it in the 1986 pavilion. The weather on a specific day in Berlin between the construction and demolition of the first pavilion will be repeated within the reconstruction on the same day every year from 1999 onwards. For example, the weather in Berlin on 3 December 1929 will be repeated in Barcelona every 3 December. The weather conditions I insert into the 1986 pavilion, such as frost, fog, snow and ice, combine qualities often attributed to the building: sensuality and coldness. All the transformations result in a temperature reduction but some are more visible than others. Snow on the travertine floor is seen immediately but the chilled surface of the red onyx wall, created by cooling elements concealed within it, is perceived more by touch than sight.

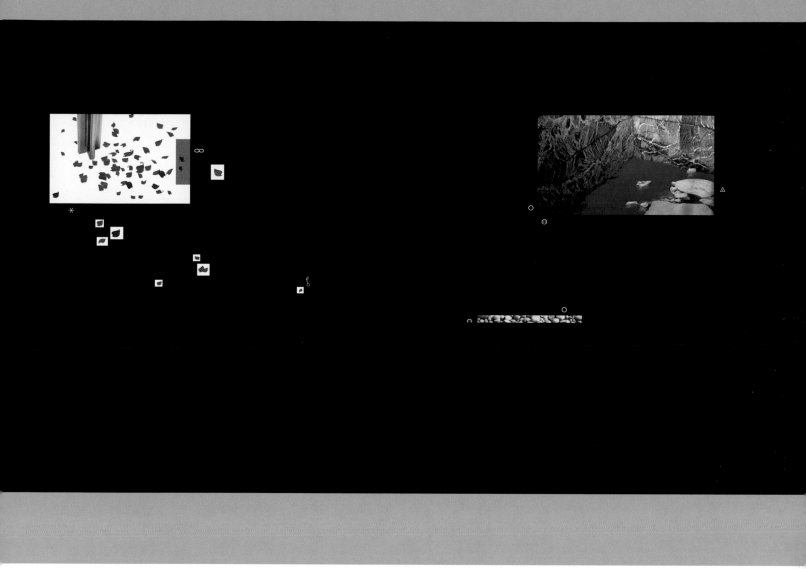

German weather is not inserted consistently throughout the reconstruction. The montage of different weather conditions within the 1986 pavilion creates an ever-changing space that enlivens and disturbs the habitual nature of architectural experience. For example, like Mies' design, Weather Architecture emphasises the distinct qualities of the two pools. On a day when the temperature in 1929–30 Berlin dropped below freezing but remains above freezing in present-day Barcelona, one pool freezes but the other remains liquid. As it is difficult to see clearly from one pool to the other, the juxtaposition is not experienced immediately, making the gap between the pools appear larger than it is, both in time and distance.

The ability of the architect to predict the form of a building is more accurate than that of the meteorologist to predict the weather, but the architect's ability to predict use is especially uncertain. However, I wish to make a number of predictions. First, the juxtaposition of the German weather of 1929–30, the 1986 pavilion, and the weather in present-day Barcelona will disturb the current experience of the reconstruction as an object of contemplation.

Second, the introduction of German weather into the 1986 pavilion will make it decay, which is expected of the building but not the artwork. Third, the inhabitants of Barcelona will appropriate and use the 1986 pavilion, and the weather within it, making it less art and more architecture.

Weather Architecture refutes the assumption that contemplation is the most appropriate way to experience the building, and questions function's role as a guiding principle in the design and use of buildings. Instead, it argues that the building that is most suggestive and open to appropriation is the one we do not know how to occupy. If constructed, Weather Architecture would no doubt be used in ways I cannot imagine. It is located within another tradition of architectural practice which, in place of the passive user associated with functionalism and contemplation, recognises the creative user as having a role as important in the formulation of architecture as that of the architect. To use a building is to alter it, by physical transformation, using it in unexpected ways or conceiving it anew. Architecture is made by use and by design. ⋈

Jonathan Hill is an architect and educator.

Notes
1. Solà Morales, C Cirici and F Ramos, *Mies van der Rohe: Barcelona Pavilion*, Editorial Gustavo Gili (Barcelona), 1993, p 14.
2. Ibid, p 29.
3. JP Bonta, *Architecture and its Interpretation*, Lund and Humphries (London), 1979, p 148.
4. Solà Morales et al, op cit, p 39.
5. Ibid, p 19.
6. Ibid, p 28.
7. The critique of contemplation is another valuable development in art.
8. Solà Morales et al, op cit, p 19.

Scene 8

When Julieanna Preston, Roy Parkhurst and Steven Marriott Lloyd were invited to submit a design proposal for the Northern Gateway of Wellington in New Zealand, they put together a scenario or installation which had designs on the ambience of the city rather than its blueprint. Mark Taylor describes how they retuned Constant's vision of chaos to become a filmic narrative of hypersurface.

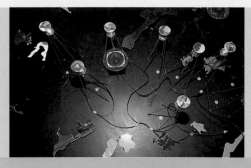
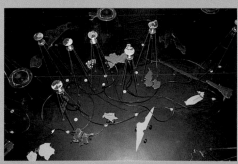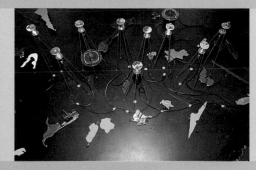
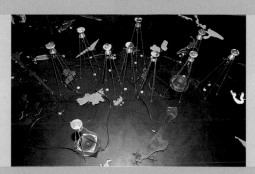

The Scene 8 project is a speculation on the
urban environment of the future. It is not a literal
urban architecture that shapes and reshapes
refined materials into concrete realities as
buildings, spaces and infrastructure, but an
allegory for 'city', influenced by narrative and
cinematic thought. As one of several participants
invited to submit a design proposal for the
northern gateway of Wellington in New Zealand,
the three-person team of Julieanna Preston,
Roy Parkhurst and Steven Marriott Lloyd
responded to the 50-year time frame and given
scenario (number 8 out of 11) by treating the
brief as any filmic scenarist would: they
imagined urban development emanating from
this story of multiple stories. This basic
heuristic device enables a processual method
to emerge and inform speculation.

However, though future trends often render
these cultural projections irrelevant, the
importance of such projections is that they
lie between cultural formations and offer
speculative thought that extends beyond

prevailing conditions. They challenge the present and
offer visionary models for the future. Inasmuch as the
given brief anticipated an urban architecture shrouded
in utopian conventionalism, Scene 8 acts as a reminder
of how archaic these forms of practice are when issues
of contemporary culture, place and technology are
approached.

Like Constant's New Babylon, Scene 8 inhabits
a space of corresponding simulation in the form of
a machine or 'game' that imagines a new urbanism
in logical operations of chance, coincidence and other
generative methods. The logic is narrative. The story
of city life – its social and urban milieus – is informed
not by buildings and streets but by and through the
characters that inhabit, visit and interact with them.
This is in a narrative sense as the project plays with
everyday lives in the city of tomorrow. Various voices
are heard telling their stories in the audio component
of the installation. And since the liveable city is not
to be found in the shape and materials of its buildings,
Scene 8's cinematic image is dedicated to the
ambience of lived experience.

Chance operations and game systems generated

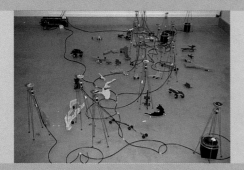
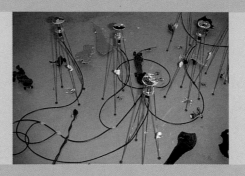

large amounts of material, including characters, their wanderings and the installation model. As distinct from the psychogeographic maps of Guy Debord and Asger Jorn, Scene 8's psychogeography of the city establishes virtual fictions – the story of the city that the project brief neglected to address. However, though patterns of association and identity are not formally articulated, characters were found through the intersection of spatial coordinates and bodies in motion. In tracing psychogeography's origins in the wanderings and irrational representations of the surrealists and following it into the work of Asger Jorn, Constant and others in the 1950s, the project has enabled a form of countermodernist revision of urban design. It is one that directly challenges the administered urbanism of the project's given 'Corbusian' scenario, and rejects any notion of 'master plan' – whatever the political, social or philosophical reasoning entailed in these concepts. Such decisions either promote strategies and motives above

built edifices or redirect those strategies for consideration in the design of deep programming, temporal zoning and systems of haptic inhabitation.

In the project brief 'gateway' was recognised as a traditional, divisional, structural and spatial marker imposed upon the city to formally define difference. The Preston/Parkhurst/Lloyd installation rejects this view in favour of a more fluid understanding of the future city, in which this city sector is dominated, dependent on and subjected to an avalanche of digital media and technological innovation. Software not hardware. Here, then, is a simulation based on the input of geographical, economic and social data, a massive hypersurface projection of virtual fiction, distilled into a representation, a schematic or diagrammatic concept, of its futures. This narrative and historical movement was conceptualised as a work of cinema, created out of a series of scripts for characters in the city, its ambience built up through an urban *mise en scène* of sound and image. These fragments of a diegesis give hints of a new urban and cultural formation, an alternative to that which is deterministically justified in modernism. Constant's

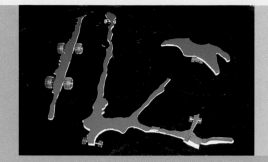

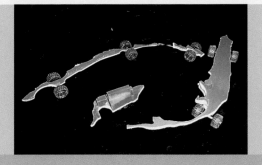

spreading chaos is replaced by a filmic hypersurface.

Colours are assigned to characters, and each is randomly dripped over the given city model while the narrative is read. Each drip corresponds to identifiable urban and landscape features in the city and narrative, so each colour is a narrative. Numerous red, yellow, blue, orange and green sectors are dissected and released from the prescribed model as fragmentary sectors to be valued, while all remaining grey areas are lost. Each character now has several coloured sectors, indicating the spatiotemporal discontinuity of the narrative. Towers appear at the narrative overlaps. Blinking and babbling they act as transmitters, communication nodes, through which characters pass and in which they are found. The old coffee-drinker, the tale spinner, gate-crasher, Sinologist and urban security officer recount their stories and settings against a background of ambient sound. Both tracks are randomly interspersed and projected through speakers

at the base of selected towers. Wires and cables snake across the floor acting as graphic markers and connect tower to power.

Effortlessly drifting, like a giant avant-garde revolutionary *flâneur*, this installation campaigns for the fluidity of the city, not its charm. It is not a city design, but it has designs on the city inasmuch as the ambient wheeled/mobile sectors do not suggest that the city is physically mobile but are concerned with shifting in a cultural geography sense. By addressing place, narrative and nomadism it alerts people to their own imprisonment within urban conventions and the one-to-one correspondence of representation. Hence Scene 8 is laid out on the floor, a rejection of the confines of traditional display models and appropriate for a new *mise en scène*. A black rectangle contains towers and painted sectors that navigate and inhabit the surface. It is both model and origin. To engage with this 'black sector' is to enter the narrative. ∆

(With thanks to Roy Parkhurst and Julieanna Preston for their collaborative assistance with the text.) Mark Taylor is an architect and educator.

Opposite
Character narratives
released from site.

Above top
Preliminary installation.

Above bottom
Tower transmitters
from above.

Fruin Street,

Millennium Space, Possilpark

In 1996, Glasgow 1999, UK City of Architecture, organised the 'Transformations on the Edge' workshops. Designed to create new public spaces for Glasgow neighbourhoods, the sites identified for the project were to be derelict and undeveloped. At the heart of the project was the collaboration between Glasgow 1999, local housing associations and communities to commission art, architecture and landscape architecture of the highest quality and participate in their design and creation.[1] The intention was to provide the housing associations with the means to develop peripheral areas to the standard of urban transformation normally found within the city centre by pairing each group with a team of designers, landscape architects and artists.

The area chosen in Possilpark, nicknamed 'FAB Square' because of its close proximity to Fruin, Ashfield and Bardowie Streets, once had the reputation of being one of the most deprived areas in Glasgow. Over the last 10 years it has pulled itself back from the brink, following a refurbishment and new building programme by Hawthorne Housing Co-operative.

Zoo Architects' brief was to design an unusual and challenging play space for children of all ages, on the site of a disused bowling green, which would provide a focus and entrance for Hawthorn Housing Co-operative. The brief was developed in close consultation with the co-operative and the local community, using a series of events to create greater community awareness and support for the project.

Initial concept ideas were tested with a strange clay model that was refined into a sketch model. Computer-generated three-dimensional models were used for a slide show to communicate the ideas to local primary children, a generation familiar with Play Station and computer-game imagery. The images were projected on to a screen on site to allow wider community participation and comment. A series of workshops were held with artist David Shrigley and local schoolchildren to form the basis of the artwork for the play area. Once all the ideas had been collated a final model was produced to explain how the space would work. This was used as the basis for a feasibility study and funding applications.

The housing co-operative suggested that the site should appeal to 'dangerous kids' and this informed much of the design. The strategy was developed to create intentional contrasts and tensions to challenge the ideas of traditional play spaces. This was emphasised by dividing the site along a diagonal axis to create a hard and a soft area, with a ramp forming a division and the interstitial spaces around the division designated as activity zones. The tension between soft and hard was created with grass and concrete, developing the theme of a 'safe' play area and a

Previous spread
Letters inscribed in concrete.

Above left top
Graffiti wall.

Above left
General view of fab Square.

Above right
3-D model of fab Square in Possilpark, Glasgow.

Opposite left
Gabion walls.

Opposite right
Central canopy and ramps.

challenging one, with structured and informal play zones. A combination of low- and high-technology play areas was used in the zones, some more successfully than others. A water fountain triggered by an infrared beam, designed to replicate water bursting out of a fire hydrant, was subject to its own vandalism, but the interactive lighting works well. The landscaped concrete provides a cycling and skating zone, with a steel skate ramp, and a climbing wall and basketball hoop. Two small play basins in the soft area provide a play area for toddlers and a larger area for older children.

David Shrigley's artwork was based on the meaning of language and encyclopaedic information which was shot-blasted into the surface of the concrete. With lines from a book of grammar, *Some Spelling Rules*, the rigid nature of the inscribed text provides a strong counterpoint to the informality of the graffiti wall. David Shrigley also created two three-dimensional pieces: a stone head amongst the rocks in the gabion baskets and a pair of stone feet on a plinth. The concrete words have withstood the efforts of vandals, but the three-dimensional pieces have suffered. On opening day the toenails of the feet were painted shocking pink, a local comment on the artwork; a year on, all that remains are the toe stubs.

The fact that nothing is indestructible has had to be faced by the design team and the client. Within a few weeks of the site opening lights had been battered out of the ground, turf was lifted and set on fire, and planks were torn from the walkway. The space still survives and was called a 'tough, tough space for a tough, tough, place' by a local journalist.[2] Vandalism and destruction have continued, despite all attempts to make the site indestructible. Perhaps the fact that the site is a target for vandals defines it as part of the community. It may be better for it to be a focus for vandalism than to be ignored and forsaken. It has been found that much of the initial vandalism was the result of gang loyalties created over two opposing millennium spaces which suggests that the space has created a sense of community and belonging, if only as an area to be defended.

The space is appropriated through types of usage and activity. Is this a situationist piece of design? The brief was developed with full community participation, the design was a response to the site and, as requested, challenges traditional ideas of what constitutes a play area. As with any public space, public opinion is divided. Local critics have branded it 'a dangerous waste of money', and have commented that it 'just attracts trouble at night'.[3] The director of Hawthorn Housing Co-operative, Susan Brown, says: 'It's the same with anything new ... This is about using space and getting people to realise it's theirs.' ∆

1. Glasgow 1999, UK City of Architecture, 1999 Programme.
2. Alexander Linklater, 'Anarchy rules no more', *Herald*, September 1999.
3. Leona Young, 'Park that's too dangerous for kids to play in', *Evening Times*, 2 December 1999.

Jon Jerde's Consuming Fantasies

and Other Urban Interiors

Jon Jerde is the architect of such commercial megastructures as the Horton Plaza in San Diego and the Freemont Street Plaza Experience in downtown Las Vegas. Projects in which he combines ambient effects – sublimity of natural landscapes, synchronised fountains and music, and lighting – with fantastical architecture. Karin Jaschke explores the 'psychogeographical' potential of Jerde's themed commercial schemes.

'Our adventure has been, to reinvent the authentic urban experience.' Jon Jerde

Las Vegas casino city has always been characterised by an extraordinary rate of growth and change. It is now so densely built up that the ritual demolition of an older hotel-casino regularly precedes the building of a new casino-resort. This temporal instability is matched by a sort of spatial wavering that becomes evident if we imagine mapping Las Vegas's casino floors, the maze of pathways, canals and roller coasters, and the strategic connections between the casino, the directional escalators, people movers, monorails and bridges. Where Venturi and Scott-Brown were still provocatively mapping asphalt surfaces and footprints of buildings in the desert, the casinos and links between them today form a syncopated, labyrinthine dreamworld through which the currents of tourists, gamblers and aficionados are flowing.

Such a cartography of Las Vegas' casinos would make for an interesting counterpoint to the maps of Paris which the situationists around Guy Debord produced during the 1950s and 1960s. In their 'psychogeographic maps,' they were giving graphic expression to the dérive or 'drifting,' a sort of pedestrian meditation on the city from which mind-clearing moments and revolutionary energies were expected to surge. They laid out carefully chosen fragments, cut from traditional maps, like a psychospatial script and established relationships between them by way of dynamic arrows, provocatively exploding the bourgeois order of Haussmann's Paris. Like an evil twin, a map of Las Vegas today would be

a reflection of the gaming business's cunning reading of the gambler's psyche and the industry's readiness to incorporate every little twist of this into the casino layouts. While the situationists deconstructed an urban fabric into a psychological one, a map of the Strip would show the reconstruction of the fractured psychological topography of a gambler's desires into a physically continuous fabric: Las Vegas Boulevard.

'Under the pavement, the beach' – and the Nevada desert

Californian architect Jon Jerde's urban projects are curiously kindred to both the psychological and economic dynamics that determine Las Vegas's growth and the various motifs which characterise the situationist city. Besides his own engagements in Las Vegas, Jerde predominantly designs large-scale, inner-city, retail-based projects which are, according to him, in the service of urban communities and civic renaissances all over the world. Critics see them as the ultimate architecture of global consumerism and Jerde as the Pied Piper of late Capitalism. This is correct on some level, but his megaprojects also represent a fascinating new genre of urban design, treating city environments as extracurricular interiors on the one hand and as a sort of urban land-art on the other. The projects are challenging for their sheer scale and offer a commentary on the state and future of the architectural profession. The off-centre location of Jerde's projects, between building collective fantasies and realising corporate business ambitions, places them right at the heart of the historically evolving dynamics of consumerism, public space and spectacle, and of the psychological make-up of the individual in the urban setting which writers from Georg Simmel to Richard Sennett have discussed.

In 1977 Jerde convinced the developer Ernest Hahn

to undertake the transformation of six blocks
in San Diego's unwieldy downtown into a 'design
shopping centre for citizens'.[1] Using a sort of
Latinising architectural Esperanto for style,
Jerde cut a modulated, diagonal passage
through the blocks and, seven years later,
Horton Plaza shopping mall emerged as a
darling destination with the public. The passage,
called 'spine' or 'armature' by Jerde, has
remained the strategic device of choice in his
office ever since. The uninhibited use of
numerous surface materials and a 49-colour
palette, as well as the excessive breaking of the
facades and floors into balconies, screens,
terraces and bridges, must have been
breathtaking even by the most daring post-
modern standards and remains so today.

The way in which Jerde Partnership
International designs what can only be described
as stylistic architectural mayhem is termed 'co-
creativity'. This designates a working process
where multidisciplinary teams are in charge of
different parts of a project. They design along
some parameter but are otherwise free to create
according to their fancy. The low-budget design-
branding for the Olympic Games in 1984 came
together in this way, based on a 'kit of parts'
and a colour palette, and appeared almost
'structuralist' in character. In the larger urban

projects this tends to lead to designs with an intricate
but essentially meaningless richness of form.

Jerde argues that the historical differentiation found
in the traditional European city centre can and must be
replaced today by synthetic complexity, to acquire its
meaning by generating civic life in the first place. As
'nodes of intensity within the large city fabric', his urban
interiors are intended to 'trigger unity out of the
dismembered, disassembled parts of the once-cohesive
city, within the abbreviated time frames of our fast-
paced world.' 'Global market forces,' he writes, 'require
that ... evolutionary processes acting on space are
completed in ten years.'

Intended as a '[vessel] for a renaissance of the
human communal scene', Horton Plaza has indeed
been alive with people since its opening. But is this
the 'public life of richness and complexity' that Jerde
is claiming?[2] With the corporate client comes a
programme which from the outset excludes a host
of 'social' functions, from kindergartens to homeless
shelters to affordable housing. However, here too Jerde
claims that the predominance of retail in his schemes
is a means to an urban end, and not the other way
round. To him, it is one financially rewarding way of
recovering territory, even at the price of this territory
being (for now) programmed, and thus reserved, for
the citizen as paying customer.

Indeed, where other architects rely on theoretical
constructs and ethical posture, Jerde uses slogans and

tactics to promote his work. His writings are
not sparkling with the sort of intellectual will-
to-power that has kept so many architects,
of his generation in particular, shielded from
professional scorn. Jerde's texts sound as
though they are written for the developer and
the layman, rather than the fellow professional
and, with regard to business, this surely
makes sense. Still, the sort of loud architecture
practised by Jerde is easily accused of
undermining the users' cultural and political
position by working into their daydreaming rather
than making space for a sobering urban
experience. Ada Louise Huxtable complained
about Jerde's 'architecture as packaging or
playacting, as disengagement from reality'.[3]

This 'disengagement from reality' as a
product of late capitalism has been discussed
by Fredric Jameson in terms of a schizophrenic
state of mind, an acute and yet unreal, isolated
and isolating awareness of the world.[4]
Interestingly, Walter Benjamin has described
gambling in a very similar way as repeated,
disconnected shock experiences, antithetical
to experience rooted in temporal continuity
and memory.[5] Neither are happy or constructive
states. However, the global success and
pervasive lure of environments such as Jerde's
urban interiors and Las-Vegas-style casinos not
only give these analyses of experience, public
space, reality and fantasy a renewed actuality
but also demand a consideration of their
'psychogeographic' potential, to borrow the
term. This is indicated precisely by the
fascinating parallels between politically
motivated critiques of the city such as
situationism and contemporary architectural
projects such as Jerde's.[6]

Jon Jerde has his own explanation of the
'disengagement from reality' which his projects
supposedly engender. He writes:
   'Each inhabitant of a city or town has a negative and
   positive fantasy of that place which is either bigger
   or smaller than real life, a collective fantasy of place.
   Fantasy about place is a primary perceptual method
   by which people form a bond with their home.
   Successful urban concepts will deliver on the
   promise of a positive fantasy in a real way.'[7]
   According to Jerde, the way to activate this fantasy
is via all the senses rather than through simple
contextual reference, and corresponds to 'experiential
design', a visceral and multisensorial variation on
theming. The users are not only being told a story but,
according to Jerde, can act out their own fantasies
as in individual movies.[8]

The use of ambient design and sensorial devices to
trigger individual imagination and collective dynamics
is common to Jerde's urban projects and to his and
other architects' work in Las Vegas. It is also kindred to
Constant Nieuwenhuys's controversial vision of a future
situationist city: New Babylon. Elaborate colour schemes
and lighting effects, piped-in scents, oxygen and air-
conditioning or the reconfiguration of the mall as an
open space exposed to sun, wind and rain, and, in Las
Vegas, the ever-changing layout of the casino floors and
of the Strip as a whole, are all catering to an architecture
of desire, addressing the id rather than the ego.

However, Constant was still demanding 'hands on'
rather than 'minds on' scenarios for the future city.
In New Babylon, '... each person [could] at any moment,
in any place, alter the ambience by adjusting the sound
volume, the brightness of the light, the ole factory
ambience or the temperature.'[9] Whereas in Constant's
vision ambiences were to be created from a
spontaneous, creative impulse and on the basis of the
New Babylonians' communal experience, Jerde claims

that vice versa the environment which delivers 'on the promise of a positive fantasy' will trigger imagination, communality and creativity in turn.

This is not necessarily undermined by the fact that Jerde's model will be fed and controlled by a rational profit- and power-driven framework. Las Vegas's gambling floors offer an instructive example of an environment which is heavily monitored, surveyed and constantly rearranged to lure the gambler and generate more revenue, but which is also a product of a historically selective process, and an allegorical representation of a form of human passion incorporating and dealing with voyeurism and exhibitionism. The question is whether Jerde's ready-made dreamscapes really have the potential to generate more than business. It is impossible to predict how possible it will be to appropriate Jerde's urban interiors and subvert their inherent social and cultural limitations and political dangers. It would be wrong, though, to underestimate the potential of urban 'high impact' projects to transform and reconfigure urban situations in unexpected and sometimes positive ways.

At Hakata Canal City in Fukuoka, Japan, rather than local references, bold geometry and large scales are at work to produce heightened physical experiences not dissimilar to the appeal of funfair rides. Once more Jerde has created a hybrid of different building types – the mall, the theatre and the funfair – to accommodate extensive retailing, hotel and entertainment facilities. They are built along a half-round canal, emphasising height while making the complex accessible simultaneously via the overhanging balconies. Deep shadows accentuate the curving lines of the buildings, which are dematerialised by the systematic use of balustrades and screens. The focal point of the scheme is an upright and open semisphere at the 'deepest' point of the curving passage. This vertical variation on the amphitheatre, so popular in the 1970s amongst architects as a symbol of, and invitation to, communality, is reminiscent of Nudging Space, a speculative urban project by Paolo Soleri, to whom Jerde feels indebted and with whom he is in fact envisaging a cooperative project.

In the same way that the prospect of an association between Jerde and Soleri, of all architects, indicates that more complex architectural configurations than we are used to might be defining the future, Jerde's own agenda has surprising aspects to it. For Namba, Osaka, the design of a large urban service-hub adjacent

to an important train station is derived from his fascination with west American canyon landscapes, which he transposes into a dramatic urban interior. This sounds like kitsch, and might well come out as such once built, but there are other projects such as Roppongi 6-6, Rinku and Dentsu headquarters, all in Japan, where terraces, water and topographical formations are used in urban contexts. Jerde's slogan-like statement that 'our work attempts to find a balance between man touching nature and nature touching man'[10] is part of the more esoteric strand of his design precepts. Although this is largely within the domain of extensive landscaping, it could be the beginning of an urban land-art that understands the city's grounds as a powerful resource and material of architectural urbanism rather than just the base for buildings or landscaped areas.

On the other hand, Jerde's fascination with the sublimity of natural landscapes and the possibility of their artificial recreation in the global city is matched by his embrace of High Tech media and, again, their potential to generate states of wonder in the user. Thus, working with Jeremy Railton, a major player in so-called 'location based entertainment', Jerde designed the Fremont Street Experience in downtown Las Vegas. This barrel-vaulted four-block-long roof in the historic centre of the city effectively turns the street with its casinos and stripjoints into a covered mall. More importantly though, Railton's Entertainment Design Corporation created a computer-driven animated light-and-sound show which makes use of the full length of the roof and explodes the space into an intense, sound-supported colour spectacle every hour on the hour. Similarly, the Bellaggio casino-resort on the Strip features an effective water-and-sound spectacle. Impressively high fountains 'perform' in an artificial lake to 'I'm Singin' in the Rain', under the burning desert sun, and it is hard to say whether the show is closer to a surreal experiment or a moment of sublime exaltation. Jerde's cooperative projects are so convincing in their use of special effects that the synergetic potential which architects have long claimed for technical gadgetry and their own work finally seems to materialise. The recognition that, where there is money, the know-how and technical means available, will allow for new ways of working with, and in, the medium 'architecture' that go beyond the ubiquitous media facade and could become a poetic and provocative part of architectural design.

At the end of the day, the question that remains is that of the future of such urban megaprojects: how will they age; will they yield to changes in programme; and will they maybe, at some point, define a new form of urban space where 'things' other than consumption – social, political, private and collective, conservative and revolutionary – can happen? This depends to no

Opposite
The Bellaggio Casino Resort. Las Vegas's splendour at its best.

Notes
1. Frances Anderton (ed), *You Are Here*, Phaidon Press (London), 1999, p 36.
2. Jerde: http://www.jerde.com/culture frame.html
3. Ada Louise Huxtable, *The Unreal America: Architecture*

and Illusions, The New Press
(New York), 1997, p 10. Quoted
in Frances Anderton, op cit,
p 10.
4. Fredric Jameson,
'Postmodernism and
Consumer Society' in Hal
Foster (ed), The Anti-Aesthetic,
Bay Press (Seattle?), 1983,
pp 111–26.
5. Walter Benjamin,
'On Some Motifs in
Baudelaire', in Hannah Arendt
(ed), Illuminations – Walter
Benjamin, Schocken Books
(New York), 1968, pp 155–200.
6. Jerde: op cit.
7. Jerde: op cit.
8. Jerde: op cit.
9. Constant Nieuwenhuys,
'New Babylon: Outline of a
Culture', in Mark Wigley (ed),
Constant's New Babylon –
The Hyper-Architecture
of Desire, 010 Publishers
(Rotterdam), 1998, p 165.
10. Jerde: op cit.
11. Margaret Crawford,
'Can Architects Be Socially
Responsible?' in Diane
Ghirardo (ed), Out of Site,
Bay Press (Seattle), 1991, p 43,
12. Ibid. pp 27–45.
13. Craig Hodgetts, 'And,
Tomorrow ... The World?,
in Anderton, op cit,
pp 188–91.

small degree on basics such as accessibility and substance. Would the landscaping survive periods of neglect or would it be dependent on constant care? Would the layout deny the owners the possibility of nightly closure or selective admission? Which access patterns are allowed to emerge?

Large monolithic developments like Jerde's are inevitably forcing architects who are willing to play into Faustian deals. As Margaret Crawford wrote in the early 1990s, when Jerde's career had really taken off: '... the answer to the question 'Can architects be socially responsible?' is, as the profession is presently constituted, no. Both the restricted practices and discourse of the profession have reduced the scope of architecture to two equally unpromising polarities: compromised practice or esoteric philosophies of inaction.'[11] Back then she suggested that architects develop a new kind of ideology, 'as positive fiction, telling a story about the larger vision of professional aspirations' in a social sense.[12] In the meantime, the Venice Biennale 2000 chose as its theme 'Less Aesthetics, More Ethics' and socially proactive

attitudes seem more fashionable once more.

However, in the debate on the future of the profession, Jerde's singular ability to attract large urban projects is an indication that an ethical premise alone will not be able to mediate between the profession on the one hand and globalisation and corporate capitalism on the other. As Craig Hodgetts notes, neither conventional planning strategies nor Jerde's teaming with capital seem to be an adequate match for the complex urban dynamics we are facing.[13] Parts of the profession at least will have to get used to working in different political and economic constellations. Parallel to that, the burdensome subject of urban-planning policy needs to be taken up by architects and students alike.

In the meantime, Jerde's projects will either inspire a new generation of megaplanners and 'co-creative' practices which, in the best case, will be able to develop a new breed of exciting urban environments or, maybe, the projects will become dinosaurs to which we will look back puzzled, as we do today to late 19th-century civic buildings in all their showmanship, and ask: 'Just what exactly were they thinking?' ∆

Karin Jaschke is an architectural historian.

Babylon

The Web is as labyrinthine and as out of control as Constant's images of New Babylon. Colin Fournier draws up parallels between the Situationist International's concept of unitary urbanism and the Internet. But how far does the situationist paradigm stretch into cyberspace?

Of all the 20th-century 'isms', situationism is probably the one that has left the least clear memory trace, partly because it took pains to negate its own existence and partly because it put more emphasis on raising disquieting questions than on providing consistent answers.

The questions were burning ones, as valid now as when they were first raised by Debord and his friends. What is the future of the city? Will it survive the wounds inflicted upon it by the scalpels of modernism? Could a radically new city be invented that would be different not only in form but also in its social and political organisation? Could a city be made of a complex network of distinct sites, a labyrinth, a series of fragmented situations, singularities, rather than the uniform hygienic models inherited from

Cartesianism? Could zoning be abandoned in favour of a unitary urbanism with no boundaries, where all activities would mix within a compact urban form? Could emotion, desire, passion, rather than the pseudo-objective demands of traffic engineering and functional urbanism, become generators of urban form?

None of the projects developed as anticipations of the situationist city came close to answering these questions and, paradoxically, Constant's designs for New Babylon eventually turned into a formidable megastructure, involuntarily owing more to the ideals of modernism than to the drifting desires of the Situationist International.

It was not in the medium of architecture that the revolutionary aspirations of SI were to find an appropriate expression, but in the explosive events of May 1968. These gave a temporary glimpse of an alternative city, setting in motion a paradigmatic shift towards spontaneous decentralised structures whose long-term cultural implications we are only now, with the development of the Internet, beginning to understand. The Net and the World Wide Web, whose invention and extraordinary success certainly have nothing to do with the aspirations of the situationists, are possibly the first artefacts to satisfy all the points on the movement's agenda, not only in terms of ideology but also in terms of structure and aesthetics.

01 The situationists asked for a city that would be conceived not as a whole but as a series of distinct sites with strongly individual identities and atmospheres. This is also the case, at least potentially, for sites on the Net and it is interesting that the same terminology is used in both cases. Web sites are autonomous entities, with no aesthetic or ethical controls determining either their form or their content, and they are totally disconnected topologically from one another, which makes them ideal situationist sites.

02 In calling for the individuality of urban sites, the situationists were in search of the unusual and the extraordinary. They were not interested in the norm, but in the exception. Similarly, the Web has no norms and, while still disappointing in its tendency to follow certain conventions, nevertheless has its fair share of sites that are at least as odd as the creations of Facteur Cheval or the fantasies of Piranesi, which were much loved by the situationists. The electronic medium of cyberspace lends itself particularly well to eccentricities, more so than the urban medium where the physical materiality and contiguity of sites, as well as their direct exposure to the public (quite apart from their functional requirements and mode of financing), inevitably impose some degree of restraint.

03 The situationists asked why urban sites should not be related to different moods, feelings and emotions rather than to functional activities. They wanted an urban topology based on love, fear, surprise, melancholy, desire. Except for the obvious titillations of its pornographic regions, the Net is still far from offering such a psychogeography, but there is nothing to stop it from doing so since it has no functional obligations to fulfill. The Net is still far behind cinema and television (and behind the real offerings of the city) in its capacity to create moods and generate emotions, but it will evolve in that direction as soon as high-quality audiovisual material becomes commonplace.

Sites will then offer emotions rather than information, as is already the case, in a crude form, in multi-user games.

04 The situationists challenged traditional notions of authorship, calling for various techniques of appropriation (détournement) in the creation of the situationist city. Similarly, the Web is quasi-uncontrollable in terms of copyrights. As is the case since the development of digital media, the culture of its sites thrives on the freedom to borrow and shamelessly depends on this for its further mutations. This is a radical cultural change which the situationists had advocated, probably without anticipating how far it would be taken.

05 The identity of sites is considered by the situationists to be more important than the medium that unites them. Their maps show sites as discontinuous fragments, floating in a void. The armatures of the city are not shown. Similarly, it would be as difficult to draw an overall map of the Web as it was irrelevant to the situationists to show Haussmann's boulevards on a map of Paris. Sites on the Web are linked by an invisible medium that is not perceived by its users. Links provide quasi-instantaneous connections from site to site, and their exact nature and configuration are conceptually irrelevant.

06 To further stress the importance of discontinuity, the underlying physical structure of the situationist city was to be a labyrinth, offering no simple clues as to location and orientation. Master plans and Euclidean geometry were to be rejected. There would be no rectilinear grid, for example, insofar as the layout of transportation systems was concerned. The Web is also a labyrinth. Its structure is not understandable as a whole to the extent that it uses physical infrastructure systems, such as fibre-optic or copper lines. These are highly complex and redundant networks with no regular geometry. It is indeed particularly ironic that, like the situationists, our most advanced technologies should pay so little respect to notions of geometric order, simplicity and clarity that were once believed to be eternal.

07 Like Internet users, the situationists rejected any kind of central political control, in their case over the city. In both cases, the chosen operational structures are decentralised. Until now, all attempts to police the Net or turn it into a spectacle have failed, and it is perhaps the first time in history that the most powerful means of communication is universally accessible at minimal cost. The fact that cyberspace, although still elitist, can escape control makes it politically the ideal situationist realm.

001

08 The situationist city, like the Net, was to be in a state of constant flux, permanently reconfiguring itself not only in terms of its overall structure but also in terms of content. While Constant's Babylonian structures were still, inevitably, relatively static, the immaterial constructs of cyberspace are totally flexible: the Web continually grows and changes effortlessly, sites appear and disappear, content evolves at the touch of a mouse.

09 Urban sites in the situationist city were to be notable not only for their distinct architectural identity but also for the events and the situations, that would take place in them. Hence the term situationism. These ephemeral situations would be created spontaneously by the users rather than orchestrated by any kind of authority. The same is true of interactive Web sites, designed as stages for events that are generated by the unpredictable interventions of the users.

10 The situationists asked for a city that would not be zoned functionally, where there would be no spatial separation of home and workplace (urbanisme unitaire). In this respect they have been successful, and the zoning concepts of modernism have been almost universally abandoned. Similarly, not only has the Net made homeworking possible, but it is potentially the starting point of a total urban revolution in that it makes all activities possible in any place at any time.

11 The sites of the situationist city were to be discovered through a process of drifting (dérive) comparable to the process of surfing offered by the Net. Drifting was to be aimless, and it is interesting to note that navigational terms are used as metaphors by both situationist drifters and Web surfers. These terms denote a mode of intellectual exploration that no longer relies on

linear thinking and neat causal chains. This also implies a form of collective, distributed intelligence, the implications of which we are only beginning to perceive.

12 Drifting was to be a playful, nonproductive activity, opposed to the work ethic. So is Web browsing, most of the time. And the Web, while offering economic rewards, certainly offers work conditions that are radically different from those that were rejected by the situationists.

The surprising and fortuitous affinity between situationist positions and the attributes of the Net does not imply that the situationist city is only likely to be materialised in cyberspace. On the contrary, what is to be expected is that information and communication technologies will radically transform the built environment of the 21st century in the same way that the machine age transformed the cities of the 19th and 20th centuries. The structure and mode of operation of the Net, and therefore some of the situationist ideas unwittingly embedded within it, will inevitably become the driving force, the dominant metaphor at all levels – symbolic, political, technological – behind new processes of urban transformation, because at all periods in history it is the dominant technology and the ideology behind it that have given shape to man's habitat.

We do not know yet what this will mean in terms of the potential future form of the city, but we know that we are experiencing the early stages of a new paradigmatic shift. The questions raised half a century ago by the situationists were early symptoms of this change, not so much because the Situationist International could anticipate the technological revolution of the postindustrial society, but because, with a handful of others, they passionately expressed their aversion to the modernist city and their desire for something else in a way that contributed to the birth of a new *Zeitgeist*. ∆

Colin Fournier is an architect and educator.

Previous page and above Stephen Tierney 2000: WEB over LA. Constant's New Babylon suggested that the situationist city would take the form of a tentacular labyrinth raised above existing towns and natural landscapes, and many radical urban proposals are variations on this theme. This project by Stephen Tierney creates new sites over Los Angeles by suspending habitable capsules on a web of cables stretching from downtown to Malibu. As a continually changing metalayer above the contemporary city, it comes close to materialising the urban dreams of the situationists.

Out of
Babylon

Barry Curtis looks at how, in Britain in particular, architects contemporary with the French intellectual situationist movement were applying their imaginations to more esoteric and eccentric effect. This was a period in which *Architectural Design* satisfied its readers' appetites for the technological, the aeronautical, space travel, and mobile and prefabricated structures.

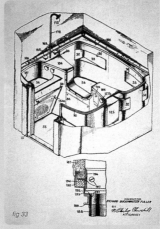

fig 33

The New Babylon project originated in a plan for providing resources for itinerant gypsies, yet was also firmly rooted in futuristic conceptualisation. A fundamental and widely shared assumption of the time was that as dwellings became more technologised they would approximate more closely to transportation devices. This would somehow have the effect of dissolving the problem of the constraints imposed by property ownership. In fact, housing became a strange heritage-related item whose values obeyed the logic of art rather than conventional commodity.

In December 1968 *Architectural Design*, in its 'Cosmorama' feature, celebrated the coming into law of 'Mr Eric Lubbock's Caravan Sites Act' which provided security of tenure and protection from harassment for caravan dwellers. It defined gypsies not in terms of race but as 'people of nomadic habit', and recognised their right to that lifestyle. Travellers in the 1980s and 1990s who described themselves as 'economic migrants' nevertheless failed to find protection under the act. In the 1960s, a nomadic lifestyle seemed a logical response to new technological capabilities. Caravans were proposed, along with space capsules, as one model for the home of the future – they were thought to be particularly relevant as they were cheap, ready-made, designed in a popular fashion and could be occupied immediately. In the same article Paul Rudolph supplied a suggestion for megastructural support in the form of a mammoth complex for Lower Manhattan into which 4,050 mobile home units could be plugged.

Many projects of the time proved unacceptable except in realms of entertainment and leisure, and the technological changes which they proposed have been assimilated in more traditional forms. Many new technologies have been packaged in ways that have been assimilated without inspiring an architecture which shared their appearance. One reason is the general unacceptability of the idea of additive untidiness and the skeletal appearance of technology unmediated by formal modification. Managing edges, handling transitions and setting in context are the valued preserves of architectural knowledge. The aesthetic challenge of neat Functional Modernism was a refusal to modulate edges, to fit in or establish hierarchies of form and to deal in the complex language of functional decorum that involved the use of mouldings, cornices and 'turning corners'. The provisional, ill-mannered and raw appearance of modernist architecture continues to be one of the chief reasons for its rejection. A key sign of professionalism is the subtle handling of edges. The issues of 'finish' and 'fit' loom large in the discourse of planning, and are specifically enshrined in planning regulations which govern the extent to which every man and woman can be their own architect.

Acknowledging where things end, and minimising the potential conflict with the things they join or are next to, involves a complex social language of decorum and decoration. Avoiding the appearance of remaining unfinished, or appearing provisional, is a drive served by an increasing range of products. Anxiety arising from edges, the incomplete and the inappropriate has been a major preoccupation of the avant-garde in the 20th century. In architecture, fragmentation and hierarchy were conceived by Lefebvre as characteristics of the urban motives of capitalism although he conceded that the system was also marked by a countervailing homogenisation, and homogenisation is evidently an important factor in masking its destructive and divisive tendencies. The *soixante-huitard* influence in avant-garde architecture promoted an aesthetic of becoming, and provisional incompletion, which aroused inevitable anxieties.

Koolhaas has described the new urbanism in which much of the landscape is neither fully private or public as a staging of uncertainty, where rules of conduct are established in the working out of economic or social compromises. As cities increasingly turn themselves inside out, their ragged edges are redeemed by mythic integrities figured in the phenomena of edge cities, malls and themed environments.

The situationists were reacting to a continuing

SUBURBAN SETS

tendency for the city to turn itself inside out, the centre shifting to the suburbs and becoming a themed remake of its former self. One of their targets was the automobile and all that it implied in terms of the destruction of the street – its conversion into highways and the beginnings of a suburban-mall cuture founded on parking space, compression and fantasy. In some respects they failed to understand the atavism involved in the dissolution of shops and streets and the return of markets, market halls, funfairs and arcades. So the situationist city attempted to exploit the density of the core whilst respecting the strangeness of the margins.

Too little has been written about everyday architecture, which can range from rebuilding a vacation home to 'knocking through'. Do-it-yourself superstores indicate a massive range of activities relating to restoring original features and there is an increasing interest in creating autonomous homes. There are constraints on what can legally be built. Planning regulations serve a number of fundamental health and safety, privacy and access requirements but, particularly in the increasingly 'conserved zones', they are a force for uniformity and 'appropriateness'. Building societies and banks have acted as a curb on the use of nontraditional building materials. One interesting loophole in planning regulations is the 'statute of limitations' which waives permission for any structure or adaptation which has been in place for a certain period of time. This has led to some interesting and unorthodox projects. The eccentric forms

of self-expression which appear on television are presumably the tip of a baroque iceberg which includes such uncanny examples as the house so lovingly converted by Fred West.[1]

Mass-produced bathrooms, pods, trailers and packages of architecture which could be bought off the shelf and plugged in never happened – the descendants of the experimental homes, which used to feature so prominently in △ and other architectural journals, are now primarily addressed to ecological ends or feature in a low-tech guise in projects to provide low-cost or temporary shelter, notably in the work of Michael Rakowitz and Wodczicko. Instead, a kind of reversal occurred in which unimaginably sophisticated computer hardware and software were installed in faux traditional buildings – often in ways that required the structures to be stripped back to their facades. The first 'televillage', designed by Ashley Dodds for homeworkers and built at Crickhowell in Wales, was constructed to look like picturesquely clustered cottages but failed to sell 13 of the 39 homes.

What does it mean to comprehend a city from 'the dark space where crowds move back and forth'[2] where the legibility of the urban text is blurred? The 'dark space' could be considered a subliminal strategy or a literal description of disadvantage. The otherly mobilised – toddlers, teenagers, the disabled, the elderly – have different relationships to the spaces of the city which are defined when they test themselves against the barriers, gradients and textures of the physical space. Polemics for alternate urban practices usually invoke a 'return' to premature consciousness of the ludic and delinquent. Outside the mainstream of consumption and purposeful commuting, those who are not 'on top of things' are the most likely to

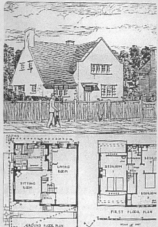

perceive the cityscape as a gymnasium or obstacle course, an intimate landscape of challenges and opportunities. They exhibit the most extreme form of Benjamin's 'state of distraction' in which visual characteristics are ignored in favour of haptic and tactile ones.

It is the people who sleep against the outside of buildings in their 'night doorways', whose attention is directed to aspects of shelter, insulation and privacy, who have the most direct relationship with the city – the most intimate and direct sensory contact with buildings and a vivid awareness of their potential for security or danger. Writers on the new cityscape, like Mike Davis and Martin Pawley, have begun to indicate how security strategies ranging from 'bum proof benches' to 'bomb proof buildings' have reshaped the environment into a free scopic zone for CCTV, minimising setbacks, heightening windows and reinforcing entrances. The outdoor realm is increasingly an area to be lit, surveyed and safely delimited. Excursions into interiors are marked by wearing badges, paying fees, swiping cards, signing in and out, negotiating with security, announcing intentions and being informed of acceptable itineraries. (*The Guardian* of 31 October 2000 announced that a strike of security guards could bring the higher education system to a halt more effectively than a strike of academics.)

Looking through the ∆s of 30 years ago it is evident that there was great anticipation of a future of disseminated architectural practice – a decentred, nonlinear, instant, disposable packaging of components for nomadic and

restless adaptors. The legacy is the temporary architecture of festival described so thoroughly in Eric Holding's recently published monograph on Mark Fisher: the climbing structures and ballparks – for people who must be no taller than a clown's outstretched arm – sited in fast food outlets, warehouses and stores in various edge settlements.[3] The recuperated ludic architecture which appears closest to New Babylon is thoroughly complicit with the society of the spectacle.

The animating force of fictional connections to the psyche has always been an aspect of the architecture of pleasure. The situationists were right in their prediction that Capitalism and urbanism would spectacularise society by supplying fantasy spaces – that the lessons of the 1960s would be learnt in the shift to self-actualisation and servicing. The desire to preserve the past has developed into a mass preoccupation, although in a reductive 'heritage' form which is clearly present as an anxiety in Debord's writings. The New Babylon persists in fragmented vernacular forms of self build and as a visual style in current architecture. People live and create in warehouses, offices, mental hospitals, pumping stations and schools – but not as acts of radical seizure. A recent television advertisement likened shopping with a credit card to sanctioned shoplifting. But it may be that sensational aspects of New Babylon have been realised in new electronic spaces, by what William Mitchell has described as 'connecting your nervous system to nearby electric organs'.[4] ∆

Barry Curtis is a cultural historian.

Notes
1. British serial killer who immured victims in the fabric of his house.
2. Michel de Certeau, *The Practice of Everyday Life*, University of California Press (Berkeley, Cal), 1984, p 93.
3. Eric Holding, *Mark Fisher – Staged Architecture*, John Wiley and Sons (London), 1999.
4. William J Mitchell, *City of Bits*, MIT Press (Cambridge, Mass), 1995, p 30.

A Global
Dérive

Gil M Doron takes us on a global journey or *dérive* of the Dead Zones of the world, in which he reveals the potency of an 'Architecture of Transgression' and documents the in-between spaces of cities.

'Transgression ... is not related to the limit as black to white, the prohibited to the lawful, the outsider to the insider, or as the open area of a building to its enclosed spaces... its role is to measure the excessive distance that it opens at the heart of the limit and to trace the flashing line that causes the limit to arise.'
Michel Foucault, 'Preface to Transgression.'

The Dérive in the Dead Zones

Singapore is not a place to go for a dérive.[1] A 'city which represents the ideological production ... in its pure form, uncontaminated by surviving contextual remnants ... and managed by a regime that has excluded accident and randomness',[2] it is ostensibly not a place for constructing different situations or for experimental behaviour.

So, instead of a dérive, I go shopping. The shopping mall is five storeys of corridors built around a large atrium. While standing on one of the balconies, which offers a panoramic view, I notice that the place is bugged with CCTV cameras, one of which is turning towards me.

Some of the shoppers who are strolling along the corridors are turning their backs to the shop windows and are leaning on the balconies of the atrium. They gaze, like me, into the void ahead. Standing there, now, for almost an hour, I realise that some of them are not interested in the shops or the atrium space. They are actually staring, through the void, directly at me and at some other guys who are on the floor below. I am staring back. The void, between us, has been cut, folded and squeezed under the pressure of our gazes. Our gaze is an architectural tool,

constructing within the void of the shopping mall a sexual playground. Somebody needs to update the planning map; the red colour for commercial use is turning pink. The commercial and architectural space is suspended, and transgressed.

The transgressive act of 'cruising' takes place within the boundary of the shopping mall's public/private space and of the architecture itself. The physical manifestation of this boundary is the void, the atrium; a place which does not accommodate any commercial activity, and which acts as a fissure within the building. Cruising opens the boundary, and creates within it

Above
The Ha'Yarkon Estuary, Tel Aviv. Only 500 metres from the bustling city, it was regarded as wasteland despite its use by squatters and for other semi-legal activities.

'a place' for an activity which is not recognised as a public one.[3] It opens up a space in the sense of fissuring an established structure, dividing it or complicating its limits ... in its transgression of the notion of place or space. It takes place for a fraction of a moment when two gazes meet, then disappears.'[4] It is an architecture of constant dérive – an Architecture of Transgression.

The Architecture of Transgression

When I drifted into the shopping mall and by chance experienced the Architecture of Transgression I had a map somewhere in my bag – a map of my dérive in Singapore, and in a further 20 cities around the world. Drawn up in planning departments, it was a (coloured) land-use map. Like Dorothy, I was stepping from the yellow to the red and blue and, like her, I found in the end, that the wizard who drew the map was pretty blind and helpless.

On this map there were areas which were not coloured in or were marked in white – 'Dead Zones', voids, no-man's-lands, *terrain vague*, derelict areas, residuum and wastelands. My dérive initially began in these Dead Zones, which proved to be everywhere but which at once have never existed.[5]

About three years ago, while working as an architectural journalist in Tel Aviv, I attended a presentation in the planning department for a new development at the edge of the town.

The architect of the new plan described the existing area as a Dead Zone. A visit that I made there, on the same day, showed that if the corpse was not resurrected it was at least in a zombie state far more exciting than the new proposed plan.

The area consists of an old port, a disused fairground, a power station and the ruins of a Palestinian fishing village between the sea and the estuary of the Ha'Yarkon river. The village has been omitted from local histories of Tel Aviv, the city that according to myth, grew out of sand or from the tabula rasa. However, the dérive in this Dead Zone revealed much more than unwritten history; it unveiled a present that was obscured by the timeless planning department's map. In the ruined village there were now squatters, including descendants of the Palestinian villagers who had legal rights to the place; the unofficial beach was used, in the daytime, by nudists for sunbathing and at night by kids for bonfires. The streets of the abandoned Orient Fair were used for public sex, while some of the warehouses were occupied by sanitation shops and others for rave parties; a disused bridge was used for fishing. Nature had retaken its place among the dilapidated streets and buildings. All of these activities happened in a place seemingly detached from the bustling city, which was actually only 500 metres away, in a place that was considered to be a Dead Zone, wasteland or urban void, that was regarded as unplanned and as lacking architecture. But that was not the case.

The constant destruction of the area was planned by the planners, along with other players in the construction and destruction of city space – politicians, developers and the local and global real-estate market. It was a zone that had been transformed into an Architecture of Transgression by its occupants: the squatters, the fishermen, the ravers, the kids, the prostitutes, the participants in public sex, who have operated in this place. They all created the Architecture of Transgression. By operating in the white zone for 'future planning', in an area in suspension, an alternative present was opened within it. This Architecture of Transgression not only changed the uses of the place, and its physical design in its local context but, through its transgresssion of boundaries, it challenges design methodologies.

The Architecture of Transgression shifts the concept of architectural space itself. That is not to say that it replaces in its wake new defined space or fixed structures.[6] 'As distinct from space, (transgression), is first and foremost not a thing but a movement of setting aside.' Transgression is 'the impossibility for an identity to be closed on itself, on the inside of its proper interiority, or on coincidence with itself. The irreducibility of (transgression) is the irreducibility of the other.'[7]

Squatting

In 1970, a group of local activists, anarchists and hippies squatted in an abandoned military barracks in the centre of Copenhagen and created the Free Town of Christiania. Now, 30 years later, Christiania is the second most popular tourist attraction in Denmark. The military barracks and its surrounding were replanned loosely by the Christianians. Today it is a kind of urban village, though very different from those found in cities in Britain or the US. It has a very mixed community made up of different ages, classes, ethnicities and sexual identities. It also has a mixture of land uses, and a unique style of self-government based on an anarchist model.

The Maxwell Street neighbourhood in Chicago, a former Jewish and black ghetto, and the birthplace of electrified jazz has been on the verge of 'constructive destruction' for the past 20 years. I met there a peculiar community of squatters who changed the face of the area by creating a community garden and public art. There is a new plan to demolish the entire area.

Top left
One of the new houses in Christiania, Copenhagen.

Top right
Maxwell Street community garden, Chicago, created by squatters.

Bottom left
The interior of 'Amerika warehouse' in the old port of Amsterdam, demolished in January 2000.

Bottom middle
Squatters' settlement in Kuala Lumpar behind the New World and Renaissance hotels.

Bottom right
Street vendors on the road to the main train station, Bangkok.

In the Dutch pavilion of the 1996 Architectural Venice Biennale the old port of Amsterdam was described as a void or wasteland, which was about to be colonised by a massive new plan. The 'void' actually contained a vivid community that included boat dwellers, prostitutes and squatters. It was also an alternative art and entertainment zone. The remodification of the warehouses by squatters was sometimes overwhelming.

In contrast to Western cities, squatting in Asian cities tends to take place on land rather than in buildings. The squatters build small houses and create settlements with the amenities of small villages. The one in the photograph is in the centre of Kuala Lumpur, behind the New World Hotel and Renaissance Hotel. It was established 30 years ago when most of the area was unbuilt. Today it sits on prime land. The other image is of the squats that line the railways in Bangkok. Again, these have the ambience of a village, though a train passes 60 centimetres away from the huts twice a day. Both these communities are being threatened with evacuation to the suburbs. Both, though, for many reasons want to stay where they are.

The planners of Mexico City banned street vendors from operating in the historical centre of the city in an attempt to clean it up for Western tourists. As a result there are now more vendors than trees in the commercial downtown area. The picture of these vendors was taken in front of the city's urban planning department building, the downtown area.

When I arrived in Bangkok the newly elected mayor publicly accused the local police of taking bribes from the city's many street vendors. Selling on the street is legal only in designated areas. However, much of this activity takes place in any available street or car park, where there is sufficient space for a blanket, a small cart or a high platform on which to display goods. These illegal hawkers had to pay bigger bribes to the police than the legal ones paid. The story was continuing on the front pages of the newspapers when I left Bangkok.

Street vendors have dominated the urban landscape since China's capitalist velvet revolution. Whereas they have been cleansed from the Western 'free market' cityscape, in China I found them in front of the holiest symbol of Capitalism – McDonald's – as well as, more discreetly, operating under the nose of Comrade Mao in Tienanmen Square. Goods are being sold from small bags concealed on the person – sometimes in men's inside trouser legs or even beneath babies. Everything is sold, from bottles of mineral water to CDs and watches.

Top to bottom
Street vendors in front of the urban planning department building, Mexico City.

Street vendors on the road to the main railway station in Bangkok.

Street vendor in Tienanmen Square, Beijing.

In the last 10 years many local initiatives by community activists have started to change the cityscape of Detroit. Squatting on and cultivating the many empty lots in the centre of the city, deprived groups have created rural landscapes and village communities on an urban infrastructure. This urban and social phenomenon is so striking that Kyong Park, the founder of Storefront for Art and Architecture, New York, believes it could become a new urban paradigm.

I found a more private gardening initiative on the disused elevated railway in New York's West Side. When I asked a woman how I could get into this garden she said it was forbidden to go on the elevated way, and continued, 'Instead of knocking it down, which they are about to do, they should create a park there, it could be amazing.'

Clockwise from top
A community garden for food production in Detroit.

A private garden was created on the disused elevated railway in New York's West Side by a tenant who lived in a building adjacent to it.

This community garden in Beijing was created illegally by pensioners on state land.

A resident in New York's Lower East Side shows a photograph album that describes the development of the garden he created on a small empty lot.

Since the 1970s residents in New York's Lower East Side have squatted in about 700 private and city-owned vacant lots and transformed them into gardens which have been used for growing food and flowers, as meeting places and for art productions and performances. The size of the gardens varies from 1.5 x 5 metres (between two buildings) to 100 square metres. In 1997 Rudolph Giuliani, New York's infamous mayor, started selling the lots as part of the gentrification of the area. The actress Bette Midler bought about 400 of them to preserve them as gardens. The rest are still struggling.

I did not expect to see a community garden in Beijing – I thought the reconstruction of the city, and the tight policing of the space, would prevent such activity. But on an empty lot, in what was the most industrial area in southwest Beijing, I found one. The area belonged to a village that used to be nearby, but had been sold 10 years ago to a private developer. As he was unable to develop the land it was taken over by the city government. In the last five years the site has been used to grow trees and local pensioners have been allowed to plant vegetables in the spaces between them.

Homeless

I met Steve in San Francisco in the wasteland area of the old harbour, which lies west of SOMA (South of Market Area). He was living with his girlfriend in an estate car among a community of car dwellers who had been evicted from the city streets. Hearing his story, I remembered the wagon community in Berlin which, from the beginning, was located in marginal space along the Berlin Wall. It is currently being evicted.

Top to bottom
A colony of wagon dwellers occupies the area of the former Berlin Wall.

The King of Mission Bay and his bus-house.

A bus used by Attila as living space, in the old harbour, Mission Bay, San Francisco.

Notes
1. Research for these studies has been carried out while based at the Bartlett School of Architecture, University College London. I would like to thank the Bartlett, UCL, the British Council, AVI Fellowships, B'nai B'rith and the Ian Karten Charitable Trust for providing finance, and Geoffrey Falk for his endless support.
2. Rem Koolhaas and Bruce Mau, *S,M,L,XL*, Monacelli Press (New York), 1998, p 1,011.
3. Gay activity is illegal in Singapore and could result in a life sentence. A few members of the gay community asked me not to mention the name of the shopping mall or to publish photographs of it in any magazine that could be purchased in Singapore.
4. The term transgression is taken from Michel Foucault.
5. See Gil M Doron, 'The Dead Zone and the Architecture of Transgression,' *Archis*, (April 2000), p 48.
6. Mark Wigley, *The Architecture of Deconstruction: Derrida's Haunt*, MIT Press (Cambridge, Mass), 1993, p 185.
7. Freely adapted from Wigley, op cit, p 73. Derrida's term 'spacing' is replaced here by 'transgression.'

In San Francisco Steve took me to visit the King of Mission Bay, who corresponded with Bill Gates about the possibility of converting some wasteland in the area into a shelter for homeless people and a vegetable farm, in case of atomic attack. He was also trying to interest scientists in the fact that drinking one's own urine could cure many diseases, especially Aids. Another of Steve's friends, an artist, who was not at home, lived in the Art Bus. Another friend, Alex, an ex-punk/anarchist girl as Steve described her, had established a settlement for about 30 homeless people on the concrete slabs on a hill above an expressway. The community divided the zone into a long-stay accommodation area where permanent shelters could be built, a visitors' area for tent dwellers and a toilet area, garbage site, etc. ⌀

Gil Doran is a writer and artist.

The Indeterminate
Utopia

Simon Sadler describes how the Situationist International was foremost among the movements of the mid-20th century that challenged fixity and historicisation, responding to the rigidity of programming and zoning of postwar European urban planning.

Historically, New Babylon can be seen as part of a breakaway from fixed structure that characterised avant-garde movements and progressive thinking after the Second World War. It was after 1945 that earlier vanguards, gravitating around the Modern Movement in architecture, and Communism in social practice, could be seen to have shifted from the cultural periphery to the cultural centre, in the process losing their promises of liberation to inure into doctrine.

The alternative posited by the avant-garde was a trend towards the indeterminate – unfixed ideologies, modes of living and architectures. It was thought possible to reintegrate culture by crossing intellectual, physical and disciplinarian boundaries. Different groups and thinkers pursued disparate, often incompatible, indeterminate utopias: some left-wing, some more right-wing, some based on economics, others on pure creativity.[1] But the situationist vision, as manifest in Constant's New Babylon, was uniquely powerful: to recover from the separated, alienated, zoned and 'spectacular' world an experience of authentic, open-ended living.

In their most experimental phases, designers from Constant's architectural lineage devised philosophies of infinite, indeterminate and provisional structures and space: Frederick Kiesler worked on his Endless City and Endless House projects from the 1920s to the 1960s; in the 1920s the designers around De Stijl, some of whom Constant met in the 1950s, offered a newly elastic demarcation of space (Theo van Doesburg refused in his Cité de Circulation, 1924–29, to remake cities anew 'because we do not know in which direction life will develop');[2] and shortly after Constant began work on New Babylon, Nicholas Habraken proposed in his book *Supports: An Alternative to Mass Housing* (published 1961) to provide only architectural infrastructure and leave infill a matter of the occupants' free will.

Previously regarded as an inconvenience to the rational functioning of society and space, human variables offered a new challenge for progressive architecture, just as western intellectuals and artists were frantically disengaging with scientific, Leninist Marxism while continuing to seek alternatives to Capitalism. Situationism (focused around the Situationist International, 1957–72, of which Constant was a founder member), was foremost amongst the movements involved in this disengagement from fixity and historicism, though at the same time it remained convinced of the possibility of recovering the original utopian impulses of Marxism and Modernism. It is the political dimension of situationist thought that clearly distinguishes New Babylon from the mere aesthetic contemplation of architectural animation that can be traced from the Gothic to the experiments of the 1920s with space-time.

The situationist project was intended to counter the extraordinary inertia that had beset the mainstream Left through Stalinism, socialist realism and ignorance of issues of everyday life and microcosmic social change. A new sensibility was marked in the 1946 publication of *Critique of Everyday Life* by Henri Lefebvre, an early mentor to the situationists and an increasingly close friend to Constant.[3] The tragedy was that leftist critique had stagnated in tandem with everyday life itself: contemporary life, the situationists argued, had become rigidly structured to the point that experience was zoned and compartmentalised. Systematic alienation was integral to a separated society (situationists argued) in

which no one was capable of understanding society as whole, nor of taking the self-managed action necessary for the improvement of everyday life. Life, they argued, was now witnessed as a mere 'spectacle', broadcast by the media, organised by the techniques of urbanism and mediated by the commodity. In the meantime, a larger, more fully lived, more organic sense of being became more and more remote.

Attacks upon specialisation and elitism had a disarming resonance for architecture, a practice which, through institutions like the ...Ècole des Beaux Arts, had been incorporated as an academic discipline, and which since the 19th century had steadily legislated itself as a profession. And Modernism's extension through town planning to the larger urban realm was like a diagrammatic representation of the forces of functional separation – housing, work, recreation and traffic, to use CIAM's famous 'Four Functions' of 1933 – a Cartesian fixation that outlawed space for any nonprogrammed activity, while accelerating the circulation of labour and commodities into a circle of productivism. The postwar planners of urban reconstruction, notably in Paris, increasingly in Amsterdam and to some extent London, seemed to the situationists to have outlawed the space for any non-programmed activity, zoning the city and obsessively improving the circulation of traffic.

The separation ensured by the urban spectacle would, the situationists claimed, eventually give way to their own revolutionary 'unitary urbanism', a city united spatially and socially by the absence of alienation, and divided only by a playful frisson between competing

desires. Architecture would no longer be the product of paid labour but would be made by all its inhabitants and users, who would be continuously engaged in a dialectical struggle between consciousness and the material world. The tendency to regard the city primarily as an object of vision could be countered by treating it as a sort of text, or as something cognitively mapped. Hence the situationists' habit of 'drifting' through cities (Paris for the time being, New Babylon in the future), transgressing the city's zoning of space and activity, creating a new indeterminacy of urban experience graphically represented in 'psychogeographic' maps and reports. 'Classic' Modernism had assumed that architectural revelation would be achieved by contemplation of the fixed and ideal architectural object, but situationism promoted architecture as an event and situation which could only be realised by the active involvement of the subject.

It was a supposition that would become generally accepted by avant-gardes in the 1960s – Archigram, Coop Himmelblau, Haus-Rucker-Co and Utopie preferring to put architectural objects at the free disposal of the citizen rather than the other way round. But situationist architecture reinstated architectural experience more radically as something in an unseparated, perpetual state of becoming. Just as the psychogeographer stumbled upon places in Paris and Amsterdam that still felt organic rather than spectacular, then so would New Babylonians replicate such situations and places for themselves. Architecture would stimulate an emotional drift from the rational to the revolutionary, putting the drifter at odds with the pretence that the modern city had ended all the struggles with objects, the body, space and social class. This sense of perpetual existential encounter was apparent in the violent drawing and scarred models of New Babylon.

An emphasis on art as a lived, playful process whose objects, when they existed, were not representations of the ideal and final but traces left behind by processes, had been a noticeable trend in the avant-garde of the 1950s and 1960s. One could see it most graphically in Jackson Pollock's drip paintings, in performance art and, most pertinently, in the creations of one of the originating groups of the Situationist International: COBRA. The intellectual sources of spontaneous creativity and living lay in dadaism and surrealism, and in postwar Sartrian existentialism, which insisted that life is negotiated, not preprogrammed.

But how to devise an architecture that could sustain and stimulate ceaseless, playful accretion? Situationists were not the only critics of the triumph of classic, static Modernism: sensibilities amongst young architects had been steadily shifting since the 1950s when, through the work of Alison and Peter Smithson and Team 10 in particular, an earlier phase of modernist theory had

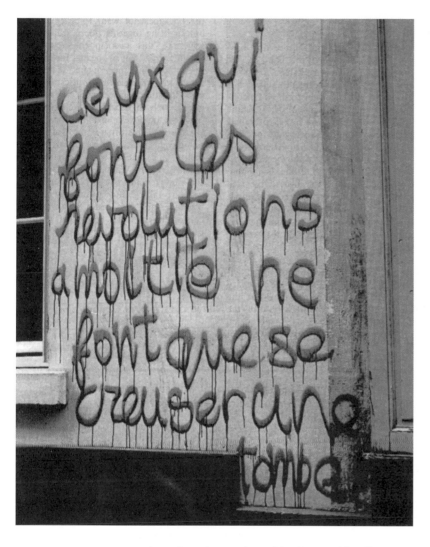

technology, which recurs in New Babylon, had been shared by the functionalists of the 1920s and 1930s. The Bauhaus in its functionalist phase had come close to an engagement with the techniques of industrial production and panel systems. Systems steadily gained acceptance after the war as an option for efficiency and economy; in the space-frame system of Konrad Wachsmann, giant aircraft hangars were assembled from standard struts and connectors; Walter Gropius, too, developed a packaged house system in collaboration with Wachsmann. Jean Prouvé worked from the mid-1940s onwards to transfer the logic of the car production line into the creation of prefabricated housing. Believing that technology increasingly delivered 'more for less', the cult hero of progressive, engineered architecture, Richard Buckminster Fuller, espoused 'ephemeralisation', in other words more performance for less weight and material. In Ezra Ehrenkrantz's SCSD school system (1960),[4] the frame became a 'well-serviced shed', a 'neutral technological frame'[5] that nurtured an infinitesimal number of permutations of modular architectural elements and servicing requirements slotted inside.

The dream of a 'floating' architecture was described impressionistically back in 1943 by Sigfried Giedion, José Luis Sert and Fernand Léger in their essay on 'New Monumentality':

> Modern materials and new techniques are at hand,
> light metal structures ... panels of different textures,
> colours, and sizes; light elements like ceilings which
> can be suspended from big trusses covering
> practically unlimited spans ... mobile elements,
> changing positions and casting different shadows
> when acted upon by wind or machinery, can be the
> source of new architectural effects.[6]

Few designs captured the vision better than Constant's. For some time he sought cooperation with other artists and designers willing to create the city as a total, mobile work of art: he joined the Liga Nieuw Beelden (League for New Representation, founded in 1954 to attempt to unify artists and architects), and coordinated activity with Spatiodynamic, Groupe Espace and Constructionist projects.[7] Constant was also associated with Yona Friedman and GEAM, the 'Mobile Architecture Study Group' (founded 1957), which included such 'High Tech' luminaries as Paul Maymond, Frei Otto and Eckhard Schulze-Fielitz. But many of these associations retained commitments to rationalism so New Babylon was unmatched in its urge towards anarchic festivity, even by Cedric Price and Joan Littlewood's famous Fun Palace proposals of 1964.

Constant and the situationists were in tune with an epoch concerned with the liberation of the mind and body. New Babylon represented an architecture so powerful that it would work directly on the body, looking to cybernetics to improve the interface between humans

Opposite
Paris, 1968. Photograph from *Leaving the 20th Century: The Incomplete Work of the Situationist International*, Free Fall Publications, 1974.

This page
'Those who rebel by half only dig their own grave.' Graffiti featured in *Leaving the 20th Century* to illustrate the article 'Instructions for Taking Up Arms', first published in the *Internationale Situationniste*, no 6, 1961.

been largely terminated by the consideration of how human communities actually function, rather than how they should function. Constant was well aware of these developments via his one-time cobra associate, Team 10 architect Aldo van Eyck. But the short-lived collaboration between Constant and van Eyck highlights the difference between Team 10's attempt to reinstate the deep structures of culture and human association and the situationists' indeterminate utopia, a vision that subscribed to no pre-existing mode of behaviour or environmental structuring. New Babylon can be seen as marrying Alison and Peter Smithsons' wandering plans (see, for instance, the Haupstadt Berlin competition proposal of 1956) with another strategy of the indeterminate, an internal flexibility and, furthermore, the possibility of continuously adaptable servicing.

So Constant formed New Babylon, not through the ferroconcrete foundations of Modernism, but amongst its cirrus clouds of technology. The dream of a lightweight component-based

The seizure of industrial culture and its technologies was the only means by which situationism could meet the demands of the masses.

Notes
1. See, for instance, Jonathan Hughes and Simon Sadler (eds), *Non-Plan: Essays on Freedom, Participation and Change in Modern Architecture and Urbanism*, Architectural Press (Oxford), 2000.
2. Quoted in Paul Overy, *De Stijl*, Thames and Hudson (London), 1991, p 144.
3. See Mark Wigley, *Constant's New Babylon: The Hyper-Architecture of Desire*, 010 Publishers (Rotterdam), 1998, p 57, note 149.
4. Schools Construction System Development.
5. Colloquialisms that were in common use at the time.
6. Sigfried Gideon, José Luis Sert and Fernand Léger, 'Nine Points on Monumentality' (1943), in Sigfried Gideon, *Architektur und Gemeinschaft*, 1956, Trans *Architecture, You and Me*, Harvard University Press (Cambridge, Mass), 1958. Reprinted in Joan Ockman and Edward Eigen (eds), *Architecture Culture 1943–1968: A Documentary Anthology*, Columbia Books of Architecture/Rizzoli (New York), 1993, pp 29–30.
7. For more information on these contacts, see Wigley, op ci., pp 22–6.
8. Quoted in Nathan Silver, *The Making of Beaubourg: A Building Biography of the Centre Pompidou, Paris*, MIT Press (Cambridge, Mass), 1994, p 41.
9. See Bernard Tschumi, 'The Environmental Trigger' in James Gowan (ed), *A Continuing Experiment: Learning and Teaching at the Architectural Association*, Architectural Press (London), 1975, pp 89–99.
10. Thanks to Barry Curtis for this observation.

and machines. The extreme refinement of the control systems of New Babylon would permit a symbiotic, ever-evolving relationship between people and architecture. Many situationists, however, were unsettled about the overtly technological direction Constant took with the project. The role of the machine in the liberation of 'the people' became a heated debate in early issues of *Internationale situationniste* (the situationist journal) and had come to a head by the journal's fifth issue at the end of 1960. Constant, who wasted no time in getting technology on to the situationist agenda, argued that the seizure of industrial culture and its technologies was the only means by which situationism could meet the demands of the masses. He was not the only situationist to harbour such 'futurist' beliefs, but (during a complex internal creative-political dispute within the Situationist International) situationist organiser Guy Debord, initially enthusiastic about New Babylon, began to demand that situationism be understood less as an agenda for urbanism, but as its critique. Following Constant's resignation from the Situationist International in 1960, Debord clung to a purer situationist idea of détournement ('diversion'), advocating the seizure and reordering of the products of bourgeois society rather than the creation of new ones, a tactic at its most devastating in the 'diversion' of Paris's Latin Quarter and the Sorbonne in May 1968, actions in which situationist personnel and ideas were implicated.

After 1962, the Parisian core of the Situationist International officially rejected art and design as part of its revolutionary programme; the task of taking culture to the streets, it was decided, had to concentrate on the formation of effective propaganda and revolutionary tactics for the takeover of the city and its economy. In Paris in 1968 the only plastic works of art were the graffiti and the revolutionary posters, and the only new architecture was the erection of the barricades, which allowed insurgents to take over the Sorbonne and its surrounding streets. Art and architecture, it seemed, were only implements in the hands of the revolutionary.

It seems impossible to say whether New Babylon was projected as the architecture that would provoke social change or whether it was envisaged as the result of social change. In which case, does not the unrealised New Babylon, the beguiling phantasm that grew through models and drawings rather than built space, risk functioning as a spectacle, as a therapeutic vision? Somehow not: New Babylon is so obviously incomplete, even visually elusive, without its attendant social revolution that it functions in the best utopian tradition, a proposition that provokes critical assessment and observation.

Yet the relationship between architecture and event has become further rarefied since New Babylon. Those architectures that have New Babylon in their blood – those themed, disjunctive, dynamic, unstable looking works from the High Tech and Deconstructivist stables – have functioned more iconographically than politically or behaviourally: they are representations and simulations of architecture as a process. In the aftermath of 1968, Piano and Roger's Pompidou Centre became an immediate focus for acrimony as radical cultural theory was recuperated into official French urban policy. As the Jury Report for the Pompidou Centre put it in 1971: '… if in certain epochs one found it necessary to hate 'movement that displaces lives' and to look for the canons of an immobile beauty, our time loves movement, and even the boiling-over of life.'[8] Despite the semiutopian ambitions of the centre's designers and managers, it unavoidably functioned as a monument to the state and its beneficence. Bernard Tschumi meanwhile embarked on a search for what he called 'the environmental trigger'.[9] But the aspiration again became frozen as an image, at the Parc de la Villette, its 'random' elements held in place by the grid, much as the free plans of Mies van der Rohe and Le Corbusier were.

Constant chose to abandon architecture in the early 1970s whereas, amongst the architectural community proper, an affection for architecture tended to be more enduring than the call for absolute resistance to bourgeois spectacular society. Spontaneism reverted to its role as a rejuvenator of form, or at best resurfaced in Punk. Visible, too, were stern, constructivist influences, indicative perhaps of the rediscovery of the 1920s/1930s-style 'commitment' of Benjamin, Lukács and Gramsci, which helped settle the bewilderment in Marxist activism and theory that accompanied the collapse of 1968 and Western economic 'plenty'.[10] Have true New Baylonians now returned, or is current interest in the phenomenon limited to the forms and effects of kinesis and impulse? ∆

Simon Sadler is an architectural historian.

Multi-Source Synthesis: Deli

Sustainable master planning and building technology need to be a comprehensive integrated process across all resources.

For more than three years between 1994 and 1997 engineers and landscape architects Battle McCarthy wrote a regular column, 'Multi-Source Synthesis', in *Architectural Design*. These writings, which were seminal for the exploration of new technologies in architectural and environmental design, are shortly to be compiled in a new anthology of the office's ideas and work, *Sustainable Eco-Systems: The Work of Environmental Engineers*. Here as a prelude to its publication by Wiley-Academy at the end of 2001, ∆ has undertaken a new two-part series from Battle McCarthy.

Below
Diagram demonstrating the relationship of multidisciplinary
engineering criteria and elemental forces that can provide a rich
platform to create exciting solutions towards a sustainable future.

vering a Sustainable Future

As designers and engineers of environments, our remit
extends beyond the design of the building fabric itself and
engages with the elements. We require a directed
multidisciplinary and interdisciplinary approach, which creates
a rich palette of tools to propose solutions towards a
sustainable future.

Unintegrated design wastes our precious energy, material
and skill resources. No matter how efficiently we design each
component of our built environment, we can only make real
improvements through an integrated approach.

We need to re-evaluate and redefine understandings of

value, in order to equip ourselves to respond to change
and to reconsider how projects are measured as 'best
value'.

The following examples are specific aspects of
projects that allow us to discuss how we can start to
deal with the complex nature of defining a basis for
creative solutions for a sustainable future. These
elementally deal with forces: wind, water, solar, skills.
Although the projects are not solely about these
elements, they are useful to highlight how they have
been used to produce an integrated solution.

Wind-Powered Ventilation

Project: Haute Vallée School, Jersey, Channel Islands
Architect: PLB Architects

We now have a much better understanding of wind data from analysis of the air-travel industrie analytical data, wind tunnels and computer analysis. These wind studies have been important in developing a possibility of an aerodynamic architecture.

Understanding of regional weather patterns and microclimates allows us to design buildings whose orientation and massing of form takes advantage of wind as a natural resource for saving energy in terms of ventilation. Energy generation can also be provided by wind turbines.

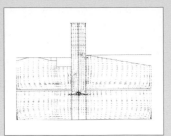

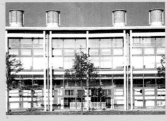

Clockwise from above
1. Model study of the site, to test orientation and massing and develop using prevailing winds to take advantage of passive technological design.

2. CFD (computational fluid dynamics) analysis. Computer simulations are produced to model and test different criteria.
3. Wind towers provide controllable natural ventilation.

Water as a Liquid Asset

Project: Rare Headquarters, Twycross, UK
Architect: Feilden Clegg Bradley Architects

The water cycle deals with two sources of water: the sky and the ground. The water is an asset as a form of potential and kinetic energy which can be used to provide 'warmth' or 'coolth'.

The rainwater is collected, filtered and treated, and is used within the functions of the building or to irrigate the landscape. The water then proceeds to the lake and then into the ground. The lake provides evaporative cooling and light reflection as well as sound.

When the water is taken from the ground there is a temperature difference which can be used to moderate the climate of the building. One method is to use the water for evaporating cooling.

The building harmonises within this process, and forms a completion of the water cycle.

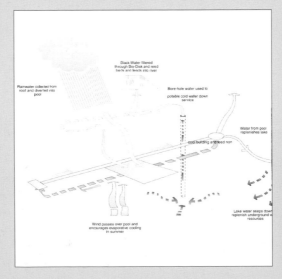

Clockwise from above
1. Diagram showing the cycle of water from the sky and the ground, and how a building can harmonise within this cycle.
2. Water channel within the landscaping around the building.
3. Lake as a rainwater collector.

Solar Heating

Project: Greenwich Millennium Village, Greenwich Peninsula, London, UK
Architects: HTA/Ralph Erskine

Solar-enhanced design works at different scales. The proposals for Greenwich Millennium Village were developed by modelling solar and view analysis. The solution was to create criteria to enhance solar gain and river views, maximise solar penetration and optimise wind protection – a strategy for facade design, planting and landscaping.

This evolved the design into a series of courtyards, modelled on the idea of the London square, as a string of pearls around the park.

The massing of the development rises from the south-west to the north to maximise river views but also minimises overshadowing by taller parts of the development.

Clockwise from above
1. Model study of the Greenwich Peninsula site, to test orientation and massing and to develop and refine the master-planning strategy.
2. Cross-section analysis, to communicate to the design team the overall concepts of solar utilisation.
3. Isometric drawing demonstrating flexibility in facade design in response to spatial adaptability and environmental design.

Precision Engineering Zero Defects

Project: Elephant and Castle Redevelopment, London, UK
Architects: KP Architects, Foster and Partners, Ken Yeang, HTA, Benoys

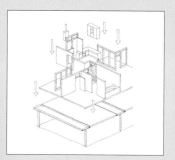

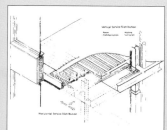

A precision engineering approach creates and adds value to a development. Previously high land costs have been balanced against cheap construction with little regard for engineering performance, especially with regard to acoustic isolation, daylight and adaptability. The redevelopment of the Elephant and Castle is based on raising values not only through environmental improvement but also through the quality of construction.

We have an opportunity to bring value to a development, based on the quality of the engineered solution. In order to bring this quality, a refinement and efficiency of how the elements of the building are brought together are necessary.

The ecological aspects of a fit-for-purpose design minimises waste, maximises quality and aids efficiency not only in the process of assembling a building but also in its performance in use.

Clockwise from above
1. Perspective sketch showing overall master plan of the Elephant and Castle area of London.
2. Prefabricated engineered elements are modularised and coordinated to minimise waste and maximise speed of construction.
3. Isometric detail showing the relationship of a coordinated engineered solution of superstructure, floors, ceilings and external envelope.

Delivering a Sustainable Future
An Integrated Approach

Below
Both sustainable urban master planning and building engineering require a wide variety of issues to be integrated in order to produce goals of sustainability.

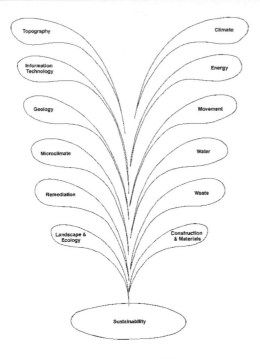

Urban Master Planning

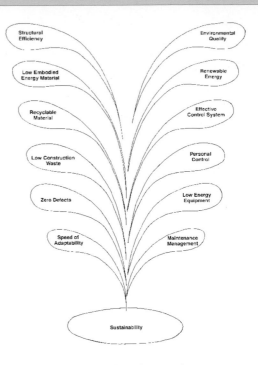

Building Engineering

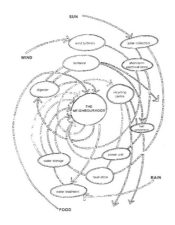

Above
The diagram represents the possibility of establishing a single community trust responsible for the construction, operation and modification of a sustainable community in association with utilities and building suppliers.

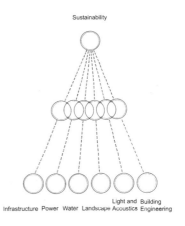

Above
Diagram illustrating complex processes involved in creating dynamic relationships between the input and output from an inclusive sustainable development.

We need to look at holistic and integrated solutions for establishing a future that is sustainable.

The value of a built environment now extends beyond simplistic accounting of its financial value – an educated public demands not only quality but also social and environmental responsibility. The development of solutions arises out of the overlapping and integration of disciplines and expertise.

As we learn more about the possibilities of sustainable solutions, further work is required in producing intelligent interaction between urban master planning and building engineering.

We need to be able to think on a macro and a micro scale, considering the physical and nonphysical, and redefining quality and value. Disciplines involved with the built environment need to understand, communicate and work with each other.

An integrated solution needs effective action. As the sustainable master planning and building technology evolves, a plan is needed for sustainable management. Establishing a community trust will ensure that the community will be run more efficiently and cost-effectively as a business. The trust will not only keep the local community, businesses and authorities as stakeholders, it will also involve the utility companies and building suppliers in a proactive steering group throughout design, construction and operation, thus meeting 'best value' targets. ◬

Building profile
The Øresund Link

In the first of *Architectural Design*'s Building Profile series Jeremy Melvin looks at a large-scale new link that joins together two major Scandinavian countries at the mouth of the Baltic. He find that the link's finesse and dignity lies not in any one innovation developed particularly for the project, but rather in the engineers' ability to orchestrate all the parts and execute them with aesthetic acumen.

If you weren't used to the idea that construction touches human and natural sciences, ecology, culture and aesthetics, you probably wouldn't be reading $\triangle$. Few projects, though, make the point as eloquently as the Øresund Bridge, spanning the mouth of the Baltic Sea and joining Sweden with Denmark. Jorgen Nissen of Ove Arup and Partners, part of the ASO consortium of consultants for the bridge, explains with apparent modesty that no particular materials or techniques were specially developed for the project. But such is the visceral grandeur of the vision that simple structural gymnastics or inventive details – those conventional badges of significance – seem trivial. The real achievement was to orchestrate the existing panoply of engineering and construction, weaving them around natural, physical and social conditions, to create a project which, in its numerous ramifications, raises a grand vision that challenges cosy concepts of Europe.

At a simple level, the bridge connects Denmark with Sweden, two countries with proud and intertwined histories. In doing so, it also joins Scandinavia to the central European mainland, appropriately enough, perhaps, given the relatively recent entries of Sweden and its eastern neighbour Finland to the European Union. But the bridge also provides an artery for intensifying the ideological debates about the nature of the union. It might also mark a shift of attention northwards; those who live around the Baltic have never seen it as less than the Mediterranean of the North, just as inhabitants of the Black Sea coasts have always known of its significance in the evolution of European culture.

If these points sound symbolic rather than actual, the bridge is also the umbilical cord between Denmark's capital, Copenhagen, and Malmö in southern Sweden, making an urban area of 3.2 million people and containing Europe's sixth-largest air-transport hub. Its designers had to consider the possibility of a collision with a supertanker or an aircraft. It is one of a series of bridges connecting the Danish islands to the mainland and, ultimately, to Germany as well. Already the region has the eighth-largest GDP in Europe, and the bridge makes it easier to take advantage of the tax differential between Sweden (relatively low personal taxes) and Denmark (a more lenient corporate fiscal regime). More than any manoeuvring in Brussels, the bridge invites transcendence of national boundaries and a return to a "Europe of the Regions". But it does not just redefine the EU. It also marks the main point of entry to the Baltic for ships to St Petersburg, Riga and Gdansk. As well as being a stimulus to already prosperous local economies, it is a reminder of a greater region where there is great economic disadvantage. And its design expresses this concatenation of different conditions. Aesthetics became an important consideration.

The mere statistics of the Øresund Crossing are not, in themselves, spectacular. It is the combination of different parts

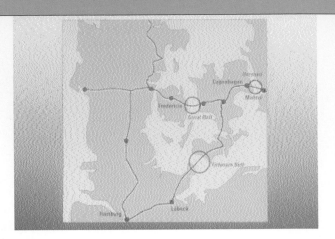

Above
View from a satellite. In a tunnel under the approach to Copenhagen airport, the link emerges above sea level on an artificial island, shaped to minimise impact on water flow, in the lee of Saltholm. It then threads its way to Sweden, with Malmö harbour visible to the right.

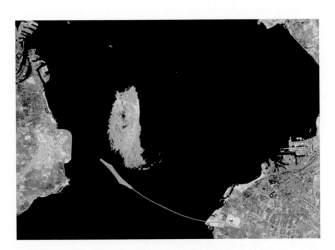

Below
With 12 kilometres above water and at 203 metres – the highest cable-stay pylons in the world – the bridge is a dramatic addition to the sea and gentle land formations on either side. Aesthetics was an important consideration in the competition, with an independent judging panel alongside those concerned with environmental impact and technical matters.

Below bottom
The cable-stay pylons are world's highest, and the 490-metre span is the longest carrying both road and heavy rail. The pylons' centre of gravity and the plane of the cables are vertical so the inner faces slope slightly outwards to compensate for the perspectival sense of sloping inwards, an attention to visual effect that a classical architect would appreciate.

Below top
The steel girders for the approach bridges, weighing between 5,500 and 6,900 tonnes each, were fabricated in Cadiz and transported by seagoing barges to Malmö where the prefabricated low-level rail deck was fitted. A lifting barge then placed them in position.

which excites attention. It comprises, essentially, a tunnel, an artificial island where the tunnel rises above the surface and a bridge consisting of two approach sections to a cable-stay structure. The total length is just under 16 kilometres, or rather, less than half the Channel Tunnel; but it is not concealed below the water. The artificial island is just over 4 kilometres; unlike Kansai airport, it cannot be seen from space with the naked eye. At 3.5 kilometres, the tunnel is not among contenders for the world's longest, but emerging on to an artificial island is unusual. The 490-metre span of the cable-stay bridge, however, is the longest such span for a combination of road and heavy rail traffic.

Social contingency rather than pure engineering dictated the combination of these components. As the flight paths into Copenhagen airport run over the water, there had to be a tunnel. Tunnelling, though, is more expensive than bridging, pointing to a hybrid solution. The link also combines road and rail, which had to rise at different gradients so they would not emerge from the tunnel at the same point. This set the length of the artificial island; ecological considerations dictated the need for the island itself. The island of Saltholm, considered a possible staging point in schemes dating back to the 1930s, had become, by the genesis of the present scheme in the early 1990s, a nature sanctuary. The Baltic, too, has a fragile ecology. Although less saline than the open sea, the flows through the straits are very important to its marine life. As far as possible, the link had to create no net blockage, with compensatory dredging as necessary.

In 1991 the governments of Sweden and Denmark signed a treaty to build the link, and the following year formed the Øresundkonsortiet to bring it to fruition. At the end of 1992 it organised a competition, and the ASO group of Arups, SETEC of France, Gimsing & Madsen and ISC of Denmark, and Tyrens

from Sweden emerged as the winner in 1993. Georg Rotne was the architect to the group. Their proposal refined the brief with an S-curved link, two islands to reduce the impact on water flow and approach bridges on either side of a cable-stay bridge with 57-metre height clearance for the navigation channel. Separating road and rail on two levels was a fundamental part of the concept using the necessary depth of the truss, while the curve made the span as perpendicular as possible to the shipping lane and had the aesthetic effect of seeming to lead to infinity. Further development saw the curve simplified to a shallow C shape and the two islands joined to form one larger one. With the concept established, ASO assumed responsibility for the bridge. Construction started in 1996.

The bridge comprises three main parts: two approach bridges with 140-metres deck-span steel girders take the road and railway up to the cable-stay bridge whose 490-metre span is flanked by a pair of spans of 160 metres and 141 metres on each side. As many components as possible were made on dry land, for economy and to control environmental impact. The girders for the cable-stay section came from Cadiz in southern Spain and Karlskrona in Sweden; the pier shafts and caissons from a dry dock in Malmö. Only the 203-metre pylons for the cable-stay bridge were made *in situ*; their 19,000 tonne weight was too heavy for Svanen, the lifting barge which placed the other components. The impact of the bridge, opened on 1 July 2000 by the monarchs of the two countries, reaches far beyond its visible range. ⌘

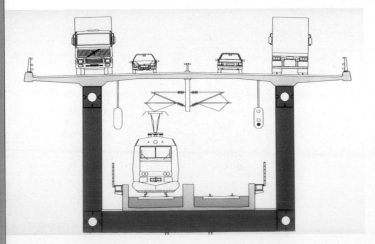

Detail of the cable-stay section girder, with fixing aligned with the cable angle. Placing the fixings at a distance from the main carriageway makes maintenance easier and reduces the risk of accidental load.

Below middle
Section through the cable-stay girders. Fabricated in Karlskrona, Sweden, they are very close to the girders of the approach bridges. Both share the 20-metre bay module, although the cable-stay section's overall width is 30.5 metres, and is just over 10 metres deep. Rail passengers are hardly aware of the change; road travellers might notice the mathematical elegance of the cables.

Below bottom
The diagonal brackets on the cable-stay section align directly with the angle of the cables, making a visually neat and structurally efficient solution. This is the first time this idea has been put into practice, although Arup's first developed it on a competition entry for the Williamsburg suspension bridge across the East River in New York.

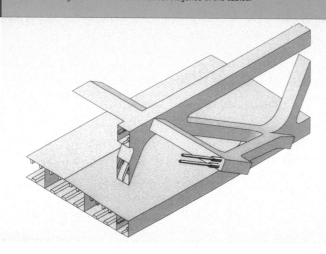

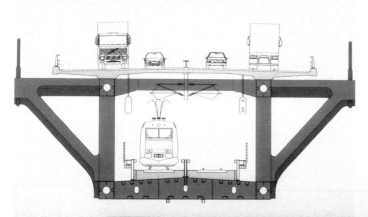

Radical Dérive

Bart Lootsma, the author of *SuperDutch: New Architecture in the Netherlands*, writes about Bas Princen, a Dutch architect who has chosen to make photographs of the landscape rather than architecture his project.

Opposite
Saturday morning, July 1998:
marble quarry near the
French/Belgium border, which
was excavated since the mid-
19th century.

Below left
Sunday afternoon, June 1998:
gravel pit in the middle of a
former commercial forest near
Oss.

Below right
Wednesday afternoon, August
1999: a former motorcycle
track between Schayk and the
nature park at de Heihorst.

The photographs of Bas Princen show landscapes that at first glance appear to have nothing whatsoever special about them. They are typical Dutch landscapes: mostly flat and artificial, entirely as if they are waiting to be rendered economically viable by some building activity or other. However, it looks as though these apparently abandoned patches of land on the urban periphery or in the countryside might have some very particular advantages, precisely because of their complete insignificance. People take them over to pursue activities which do not have a place anywhere else and would not be tolerated. These are essentially leisure pursuits, activities which are intrinsically 'useless': camping, sports, racing around in a motor boat or driving through mud in a jeep, strolling, taking a short break on a Sunday outing between somewhere and somewhere else, looking around aimlessly and, above all, doing nothing. Quite regardless of whether they are doing nothing or racing around, in one way or another the people in Bas Princen's photographs are intensely preoccupied. The self-confidence with which they occupy the countryside is reminiscent of that shown by squatters. The incredible vitality they exude is perhaps connected to the emptiness that surrounds them. The traces they leave in their wake probably disappear rapidly; all it takes is a decent shower of rain.

However, Princen is not primarily a photographer: he is a designer, and he sees this series of photographs as a project. Photography is usually only used by designers for their studies – as Rem Koolhaas, Stefano Boeri and Adriaan Geuze have done – or they employ it to document their realised projects and capture them in as attractive a manner as possible for publication in the relevant journals. Princen quite deliberately avoids using it for reasons like these. The photographs are the project itself: the studies, the design, realisation and documentation in one. He sees his photographs as a kind of legitimisation of the situations he has encountered, as kinds of ready-mades.

The strategy of simply using a different form of representation to change the perception of the existing and thereby solve serious problems is not without precedent in the Netherlands. Lucas Verwey of Buro Schie, for example, altered the view of the conglomeration of towns and villages in the west Netherlands with his map of Randstad. Presenting it as a banal street map and adding the daytime and night routes of public transport, as is done in any metropolis, made it clear that the region had long been one single city for those living there and that it was used as such.

There are more, and more specific, predecessors to Princen and his work. First and foremost, we have to think of Rem Koolhaas, who in his project for the Parc de la Villette did not so much introduce architectural elements as programme the ground in strips of different activities. Koolhaas is known for his rejection of design even though he still produces exciting buildings and urban plans. But these are mainly continuations and extensions – possibly seamless – of the ground, the surface of the earth. In fact, his whole work is a plea for a '"functionalist" architecture which is not obsessed with form, but which conceives of and creates structures for human activity in previously nonexistent juxtapositions and catalysing combinations on the floor (meaning the surface of the earth).'[1]

Also worthy of mention as predecessors to Princen

Below top
Friday evening, June 1998: a field for sheep, which doubles
up as an airfield for model aeroplanes, located between the
A-50 motorway and the Maashorst nature park.

Below bottom
Thursday afternoon, March 1998: former
gravel pit between Langenboom and Mill.

Below top
Friday evening, June 1998: a field for sheep, which doubles up as an airfield for model aeroplanes, located between the A-50 motorway and the Maashorst nature park.

Below bottom
Thursday afternoon, March 1998: former gravel pit between Langenboom and Mill.

are the situationists of the 1950s and 1960s, in whom increasing interest has been shown over the past few years. The way in which people utilise the countryside in Princen's work is in truth – without their knowing it – a radical form of dérive (aimless wandering). This lack of plan or aim while cruising through the city in search of specific experiences was a means for the situationists to work out the essential aspects of urban life that were deliberately concealed, and whose existence was denied by an officious urban planning to which they were subordinate. The people in Princen's photographs do this in an even more radical form: they do not just go by foot, they cover great distances in their cars in search of intense experiences. In the 1960s, Constant, a long-standing member of Situationist International, predicted that when people have more leisure time at their disposal they will collectively develop a lifestyle for themselves that is based on mobility and play. In playing, they would use all the technological aids at their disposal to create their own ambience in a creative manner.

In the work of Adriaan Geuze and West 8 landscape architects, Koolhaas and the situationists meet. Geuze's city dweller is not Constant's emancipated, creative and playful *Homo ludens*, but the typical product of the Western welfare system: an articulate, individualistic consumer, educated and well off – one who knows what he or she wants. In Geuze's

eyes the city dweller is not a pitiable victim who has to be cosseted and protected by urban developers and landscape architects who place their homes in discreet green surroundings. The city dweller is far more somebody who self-assuredly selects the place they want to stay:

The surroundings do not have to always be adapted to meet the apparent wishes of the city dweller, the city dweller adapts to their surroundings ...The city dweller is continually changing their activities and surroundings, he/she seeks recreation in the Maas Estuary and in the Alps, relaxes in dark streets, passes through the countryside, sleeps and works in a variety of places, does not have their family and friends in the same street.[2]

In the conclusion to his programmatic text *Accelerating Darwin* Geuze hopes the new public space will manipulate its users in such a way that their behaviour becomes conscious and can no longer regress into preprogrammed mechanical acts: 'Design is no longer the issue, or the beauty of proportion, the material and the color, but the perception of loose culture, of that which the city dwellers create there.'[3]

Below
Saturday afternoon, September 1999: discotheque
car park, former tennis courts, in the middle of a
small village south of Nijmegen.

Designing therefore becomes a kind of 'giving reality an amnesty', as Laurids Ortner once called it – and this is precisely what Bas Princen does with his photographs.[4] However, this amnesty is not free from criticism: it is certainly a possible form of design, and an emancipating critique on the standard forms of architecture and planning, but it is something quite different to what the situationists had in mind. Everyday life might have been overcome, but not yet the capitalist system as can be seen more clearly now than ever. Guy Debord thought capitalism would lead to the trivialisation and homogenisation of space as soon as it became globally applied. Even more quickly than he or his followers could ever have dreamt, the system has adapted the phenomenon of individualisation and, contrary to what he expected, has helped to bring it about. For the nth time it has 'absorbed' the arguments of its own critics.

Bart Lootsma, *SuperDutch: New Architecture in the Netherlands*, is published by Thames and Hudson (London), 2000.

Notes
1. Rem Koolhaas: Unsere 'Neue Sachlichkeit' in Jacques Lucan, *OMA: Rem Koolhaas*, Verlag für Architektur, Artemis & Winkler (Zürich and Munich), 1991.
2. Adriaan Geuze, 'Wilderness' in Anne Mie Devolder (ed), *De Alexanderpolder, waar de stad verder gaat*, Thoth (Bussum) 1993.
3. Adriaan Geuze, 'Accelerating Darwin' in Gerrit Smienk (ed), *NL Nederlandse landschapsarchitectuur, tussen traditie en experiment*, Thoth (Amsterdam), 1993.
4. Laurids Ortner, 'An amnesty for constructed reality', *Forum 31-1*, 1986–87.

November 1998	Graduated Cum Laude as a designer for public space at the Design Academy in Eindhoven.
May 1999	Co-founded TJJLP Designers, Rotterdam (multidisciplinary office for design, public space and architecture).
July 1999	Solo exhibition 'Artificial Archaic Landscape', Breda.
September 1999	Received a grant to study at the Postgraduate Laboratory of Architecture at the Berlage Institute, Rotterdam.
August 2000	Exhibited with the USE (Uncertain States of Europe) project founded by Stefano Boeri for the Mutations exhibition in Bordeaux.
September 2000	Teacher in the architecture department at the Technical University, Eindhoven.

Book Review

Seeking Equilibrium

EQUILIBRIUM: The Work of Nicholas Grimshaw & Partners,
by Hugh Pearman, Phaidon Press Ltd (London), 2000,
256 pp, HB, £45.00/$75.00.

This is a book to covet. It shows the work of one of the UK's best architects, in the greatest detail and beautifully presented. Seventeen buildings are included, most of them recently completed or about to be built. All are copiously illustrated with photographs, scale drawings and concept sketches. The author's text is clear and informative, describing the structure of the buildings, how they are used and experienced and how they respond to the environment. I particularly like the personal comments with which Nick himself introduces each one.

The buildings represent a large variety of categories: offices, a chamber of commerce, a space centre, exhibition buildings, a science institute, a bridge, a spa and, last but not least, the impressive Eden Project in Cornwall. Nick says, 'This project held the office in thrall since the moment we got it.'

It is a plant enclosure, the largest in the world, set in a vast landscape once dotted with china-clay mounds and pits long since abandoned. The brief called for the lightest and most ecological solution and this has been achieved with a Buckminster Fuller geodesic structure, clusters of interlinked domes based on a nine-metre hexagonal 'glazed' module with cushions of EFTE transparent foil in lieu of glass. There are two main clusters, one is a warm temperate zone, the other a humid tropical one. Inside they are high enough to house tall rainforest trees. A visitor centre links the two.

Inflated EFTE transparent foil cushions turn up again in the National Space Science Centre under way in Leicester, this time cladding a double-curved rocket tower, a landmark for the city.

It seems intrepid to introduce a contemporary spa into a place like Bath, but NGP have done this ingeniously in the midst of historic buildings. What is more, they have put an open-air pool on the roof in addition to the pool at ground level.

At Lord's their grandstand on the north side, replacing the original one, completes the enclosure of this renowned cricket ground. It is white like neighbouring stands by Michael Hopkins & Partners and themselves and the dramatic press box perched on high by Future Systems. Lord's has become a mecca for architects.

Travellers are already familiar with some NGP buildings: Waterloo and Paddington rail stations; the RAC headquarters near Bristol whose 'crow's-nest' observation tower is a landmark for motorists; and by 2003 they will enjoy using the Zurich airport terminal extension.

NGP have gained a strong foothold in Germany. The Mabeg office building at Soast, completed in 1999, merges architecture and industrial design acting as an image for the company and a showcase for its products. In Frankfurt the exhibition hall, soon due for completion, has an elegant folded-structure roof spanning the great rectangular space. And the Ludwig Erhard Haus in Berlin, the Chamber of Trade and Commerce, is possibly the most interesting of all the commercial buildings illustrated. A bit like a large silver armadillo, it appears squashed in its surroundings but is spacious inside with two dramatically high atria carrying wall-climber lifts. The Stock Exchange below the larger atrium can be viewed from above.

Most of the schemes in this monograph are competition winners.

I could continue describing other buildings in Europe, or NGP's industrial designs, but readers will have to see for themselves how interesting they are and what a beautiful job Phaidon has done in presenting them. This volume is the third of three on Grimshaw's work.

A previous thoughtful lecture of Nick's is added at the end of the book, in which he talks about global responsibility and what architects could do about it. For further reading a bibliography is included; also a list of the many awards the firm has won. But the Pritzker and Stirling prizes and the Royal Gold Medal are not yet among them. I wonder why. ◻ *Monica Pidgeon*

Highlights from Wiley-Academy

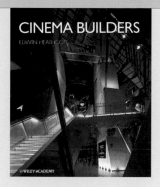

CINEMA BUILDERS
Edwin Heathcote
HB 0 471 49138 1; £50; 305 → 252 mm; 224 pages; April 2001

The cinema is a quintessentially modern building type. Accommodating a technology that has existed for little more than a century, it has developed freely, without direct historical precedent. Rooted in the architecture of the theatre, it quickly came into its own adopting a purely modernistic vocabulary, and replaced the theatre as the most significant urban leisure attraction. This book offers a comprehensive companion to the history of this building type, while featuring detailed sections on the most notable recent examples throughout the world.

In his introductory essays Edwin Heathcote charts the development of the cinema building from its inauspicious beginnings in seedy, darkened rooms and travelling fairground booths, to its rapidly achieved status as a cultural icon. In doing so, he demonstrates how changing attitudes to the art of film shaped the structures that were built to house this art, along with evolving social, economic and political factors. The basic wooden huts that housed peepshows, which constituted the earliest popular use of film, were notoriously inclined to burst into flame, and were soon superseded by a totally contrary architecture: one of inspiration. The Art Deco 'dream-palaces' of the 1930s perfectly complemented the extravagant, fantastical movies, such as the epic musicals of Busby Berkeley, which helped a society plagued by economic insecurity to escape from the anxieties of everyday life. The advent of the drive-in movie theatre in the 1950s was an embodiment of the 'American Dream' – the pioneering spirit and the love of freedom that was reflected in film by the covert anti-Communism of horror movies involving aliens and technology-gone-wrong. A reaction to the extravaganzas of Hollywood were the ascetic art-house cinemas of the 1950s and 1960s. By the 1980s, the all-encompassing onslaught of Thatcherist/ Reaganist capitalism brought into being the blatantly commercial cinema complex, which has led in recent years to numerous anonymous multiplexes.

Heathcote's full account of cinema's social and cultural history is followed up by descriptions of over 30 contemporary cinema buildings. Each project description is lavishly illustrated with plans, drawings and colour photographs. Examples are drawn from all over the world and include cinemas by Bryan Avery, Coop Himmelb(l)au and Jon Jerde.

THE PARADOX OF CONTEMPORARY ARCHITECTURE
Edited by Peter Cook, Neil Spiller, Laura Allen and Peg Rawes
PB 0 471 49685 5; £24.95; 279 → 217 mm; 128 pages; March 2001

One of the most fruitful methods of architectural education is the fostering of links between students and practising architects. This is done every year at the world-renowned Bartlett School of Architecture in London, by way of a series of lectures funded by advertising magnate Frank Lowe. Through these lectures, students at the Bartlett have already benefited from interaction with many major influential cutting-edge architects, as well as those who are up-and-coming.

This new series of books, which began in 1999 with *The Power of Contemporary Architecture*, turns this resource from a privilege available only to students at the Bartlett into a key resource for anyone interested in the development of cutting-edge architecture and the directions it might take in the future. As with other titles to come, *The Paradox of Contemporary Architecture*, which covers the Lowe Lectures given in the year 2000, comprises summaries of talks by a wide selection of architects, each presenting their work and the theories behind it.

Unlike most high-profile lecture series, the Lowe Lectures feature a rare mixture of world-renowned architects at the height of their fame alongside almost unheard-of young architects, selected by Peter Cook, Neil Spiller and others associated with the Bartlett in the belief that their work will – or at least should – soon gain prominence.

The lectures range from discussion of specific projects to more abstract ideological texts. Among the better-known architects and firms who have contributed to this volume are Claude Parent, Zaha Hadid, Stephen Perrella, LOT/EK, Zamp Kelp and Softroom. With their essays complemented by those of lesser-known contemporaries who promise to develop into the Hadids, Peter Smithsons and Cedric Prices of the next generation, this book provides a fascinating mixture of the established and the new, and offers a compelling and inspiring read to anyone with an interest in the architectural avant-garde.

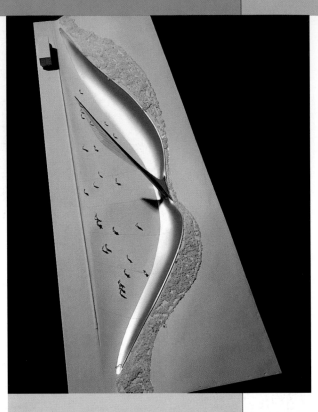

Fellow Czech compatriot and
collaborator on the project,
Ivan Margolius writes about
Future Systems' design
for a Memorial to the Victims
of Communism in Prague.

Why should an architect design a memorial? It is an object that
by its nature displays remembrance, a reminder of the past
and humiliation of the vanquished. It is a process that should
encompass architecture, art, symbolism, politics and history
into one eloquent element. In the case of Jan Kaplicky (Future
Systems' founding partner) the design stems personally from
the country of his birth, the course of his life, education and
culture, and binds him, with a duty to contribute the skill he
has, to realise creative expression on behalf of his countrymen,
cleansing himself and themselves of the troubled past.

The Holocaust memorials being erected in Western Europe
and the USA remind us of the millions of victims of the Second
World War. That a similar and even more vicious horror
continued after the war in Soviet-occupied countries
for another, seemingly peaceful, 42 years is not yet fully
appreciated. Countless innocent people were tortured, starved,
brainwashed, herded into concentration camps and uranium
mines, their possessions confiscated and their families forcibly
separated. Stalin and his regime instigated witch-hunts and
instilled fear in people in order to satisfy the paranoia of Soviet
Communism and its desire to survive. Citizens turned into an
introverted society that felt humiliated, unable to express
feelings, desires, thoughts and opinions, publicly voicing the
official views but privately doubting the value of their very own
attitudes and existence.

My parents, both born in Prague, lived through the worst
period of the 20th century. After their short youth in the
interwar years they were deported to Nazi concentration
camps at the beginning of the Second World War. Miraculously
they survived. Soon after, the Communist dictatorship imposed
its regime on half of Europe continuing the terror started by
the Third Reich. My father, who became deputy minister of
the Czechoslovak Foreign Trade, was executed a few years
later as one of the defendants in the unlawful Slansky Trial
orchestrated by Soviet advisers. My mother lost her husband
and all her possessions, and existed without regular
employment, health care and decent accommodation while
caring for a small son. There were numerous similar cases
during the 42 years of Communist rule with almost 6,000
people losing their lives and many more thousands
incarcerated in prisons and camps.

In 1993 Future Systems conceived their first Memorial
to the Victims of Communism. Cut into the slope of the
Letna Plain, it would symbolise the permanent scar
left by the suffering of the country's people. The 42
stainless-steel steps suspended over the valley of black
granite inscribed with the names of victims would be
located exactly where the infamous Stalin statue stood
between 1955 and 1962. This project, suggested
perhaps too soon after the Velvet Revolution, was not
adopted by the Czech government. Early in 2000 a
new competition was announced and Future Systems
submitted a new design, this time for a site located
under the Petrin Hill opposite the National Theatre.
Kaplicky felt that the monument should be apolitical
and that it should be an honest work and should
produce strong emotion in the observer. It should not
be a static object, but an element that would open the
way towards understanding the past. The memorial
should express the respect of the nation and be a
warning for its future. The aim of the design was to
lead the observer from death to a better life. The
memorial was set into the profile of the hill as an
extended stainless-steel shield carrying names, with
a flagstaff rising from it, symbolising the return of
freedom and victory over dictatorship. The shield
covered the inflicted wound, penetrating and healing it.
It became part of life not an inanimate object, a fitting
tribute to all who suffered and died. ⚏

Ivan Margolins is author of *Automobiles by Architects*,
(Wiley-Academy. February 2000).

Subscribe Now for 2001

As an influential and prestigious architectural publication, *Architectural Design* has an almost unrivalled reputation worldwide. Published bi-monthly, it successfully combines the currency and topicality of a newsstand journal with the editorial rigour and design qualities of a book. Consistently at the forefront of cultural thought and design since the 60s, it has time and again proved provocative and inspirational – inspiring theoretical, creative and technological advances. Prominent in the 80s for the part it played in Post-Modernism and then in Deconstruction, △ has recently taken a pioneering role in the technological revolution of the 90s. With ground-breaking titles dealing with cyberspace and hypersurface architecture, it has pursued the conceptual and critical implications of high-end computer software and virtual realities. △

△ Architectural Design

SUBSCRIPTION RATES 2001
Institutional Rate: UK £150
Personal Rate: UK £97
Discount Student* Rate: UK £70
OUTSIDE UK
Institutional Rate: US $225
Personal Rate: US $145
Student* Rate: US $105

*Proof of studentship will be required when placing an order. Prices reflect rates for a 2001 subscription and are subject to change without notice.

TO SUBSCRIBE
Phone your credit card order:
UK/Europe: +44 (0)1243 843 828
USA: +1 212 850 6645
Fax your credit card order to:
UK/Europe: +44 (0)1243 770 432
USA: +1 212 850 6021

Email your credit card order to:
cs-journals@wiley.co.uk
Post your credit card or cheque order to:

UK/Europe: John Wiley & Sons Ltd.
Journals Administration Department
1 Oldlands Way
Bognor Regis
West Sussex PO22 9SA
UK

USA: John Wiley & Sons Ltd.
Journals Administration Department
605 Third Avenue
New York, NY 10158
USA

Please include your postal delivery address with your order.

All △ volumes are available individually. To place an order please write to:
John Wiley & Sons Ltd
Customer Services
1 Oldlands Way
Bognor Regis
West Sussex PO22 9SA

Please quote the ISBN number of the issue(s) you are ordering.

△ is available to purchase on both a subscription basis and as individual volumes

---

◯ I wish to subscribe to △ Architectural Design at the **Institutional rate of £150.**

◯ I wish to subscribe to △ Architectural Design at the **Personal rate of £97.**

◯ I wish to subscribe to △ Architectural Design at the **Student rate of £70.**

STARTING FROM ISSUE 1/2001.

◯ Payment enclosed by Cheque/Money order/Drafts.

Value/Currency £/US$ [   ]

◯ Please charge £/US$ [   ] to my credit card.

Account number:
[ ][ ][ ][ ][ ][ ][ ][ ][ ][ ][ ][ ][ ][ ][ ][ ]

Expiry date:
[ ][ ][ ][ ][ ]

Card: Visa/Amex/Mastercard/Eurocard *(delete as applicable)*

Cardholder's signature [   ]
Cardholder's name [   ]
Address [   ]
[   ]
[   ] Post/Zip Code [   ]

Recepient's name [   ]
Address [   ]
[   ]
[   ] Post/Zip Code [   ]

I would like to buy the following Back Issues at £19.99 each:

◯ △ 150 *Architecture and Animation*, Bob Fear

◯ △ 149 *Young Blood*, Neil Spiller

◯ △ 148 *Fashion and Architecture*, Martin Pawley

◯ △ 147 *The Tragic in Architecture*, Richard Patterson

◯ △ 146 *The Transformable House*, Jonathan Bell and Sally Godwin

◯ △ 145 *Contemporary Processes in Architecture*, Ali Rahim

◯ △ 144 *Space Architecture*, Dr Rachel Armstrong

◯ △ 143 *Architecture and Film II*, Bob Fear

◯ △ 142 *Millennium Architecture*, Maggie Toy and Charles Jencks

◯ △ 141 *Hypersurface Architecture II*, Stephen Perrella

◯ △ 140 *Architecture of the Borderlands*, Teddy Cruz

◯ △ 139 *Minimal Architecture II*, Maggie Toy

◯ △ 138 *Sci-Fi Architecture*, Maggie Toy

◯ △ 137 *Des-Res Architecture*, Maggie Toy

◯ △ 136 *Cyberspace Architecture II*, Neil Spiller

◯ △ 135 *Ephemeral/Portable Architecture*, Robert Kronenburg

◯ △ 134 *The Everyday and Architecture*, Sarah Wigglesworth

◯ △ 133 *Hypersurface Architecture*, Stephen Perrella

◯ △ 132 *Tracing Architecture*, Nikos Georgiadis

◯ △ 131 *Consuming Architecture*, Sarah Chaplin and Eric Holding